M000233237

Plans and situated actions
The problem of human–machine communication

Plans and situated actions

The problem of human–machine communication

LUCY A. SUCHMAN

Intelligent Systems Laboratory, Xerox Palo Alto Research Center

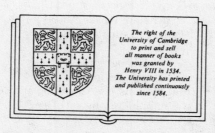

The right of the
University of Cambridge
to print and sell
all manner of books
was granted by
Henry VIII in 1534.
The University has printed
and published continuously
since 1584.

CAMBRIDGE UNIVERSITY PRESS

Cambridge

New York   New Rochelle   Melbourne   Sydney

Published by the Press Syndicate of the University of Cambridge
The Pitt building, Trumpington Street, Cambridge CB2 1RP
32 East 57th Street, New York, NY 10022, USA
10 Stamford Road, Oakleigh, Melbourne 3166, Australia

© Cambridge University Press 1987

First published 1987

Printed in Great Britain by
Redwood Burn Limited, Trowbridge, Wiltshire

British Library cataloguing in publication data
Suchman, Lucy A.
Plans and situated actions: the problem
of human–machine communication.
1. Man–machine systems   2. Electronic
digital computers
I. Title
004'.01'9   QA76.5

Library of Congress cataloguing in publication data
Suchman, Lucille Alice.
Plans and situated actions.

Bibliography.
Includes index.
1. Man–machine systems.   2. Cognition and culture.
3. Ethnophilosophy.   I. Title.
T59.7.S83   1987   128'.4   87–8013

ISBN 0 521 33137 4 hard covers
ISBN 0 521 33739 9 paperback
RB

Contents

Preface

> Thomas Gladwin (1964) has written a brilliant article contrasting the method by which the Trukese navigate the open sea, with that by which Europeans navigate. He points out that the European navigator begins with a plan – a course – which he has charted according to certain universal principles, and he carries out his voyage by relating his every move to that plan. His effort throughout his voyage is directed to remaining "on course." If unexpected events occur, he must first alter the plan, then respond accordingly. The Trukese navigator begins with an objective rather than a plan. He sets off toward the objective and responds to conditions as they arise in an *ad hoc* fashion. He utilizes information provided by the wind, the waves, the tide and current, the fauna, the stars, the clouds, the sound of the water on the side of the boat, and he steers accordingly. His effort is directed to doing whatever is necessary to reach the objective. If asked, he can point to his objective at any moment, but he cannot describe his course.   (Berreman 1966, p. 347)

The subject of this book is the two alternative views of human intelligence and directed action represented here by the Trukese and the European navigator. The European navigator exemplifies the prevailing cognitive science model of purposeful action, for reasons that are implicit in the final sentence of the quote above. That is to say, while the Trukese navigator is hard pressed to tell us how he actually steers his course, the comparable account for the European seems to be already in hand, in the form of the very plan that is assumed to guide his actions. While the objective of the Trukese navigator is clear from the outset, his actual course is contingent on unique circumstances that he cannot anticipate in advance. The plan of the European, in contrast, is derived from universal principles of navigation, and is essentially independent of the exigencies of his particular situation.

Given these contrasting exemplars, there are at least three, quite different implications that we might draw for the study of purposeful action:

First, we might infer that there actually are different ways of acting, favored differently across cultures. How to act purposefully is learned, and subject to cultural variation. European culture favors abstract, analytic thinking, the ideal being to reason from general principles to particular instances. The Trukese, in contrast, having no such ideological commitments, learn a cumulative range of concrete, embodied responses, guided by the wisdom of memory and experience over years of actual voyages. In the pages that follow, however, I will argue that all activity, even the most analytic, is fundamentally concrete and embodied. So while there must certainly be an important relationship between ideas about action and ways of acting, this first interpretation of the navigation example stands in danger of confusing theory with practice.

Alternatively, we might posit that whether our actions are *ad hoc* or planned depends upon the nature of the activity, or our degree of expertise. So we might contrast instrumental, goal-directed activities with creative or expressive activities, or contrast novice with expert behavior. Dividing things up along these lines, however, seems in some important ways to violate our navigation example. Clearly the Truk is involved with instrumental action in getting from one island to another, and just as clearly the European navigator relies upon his chart regardless of his degree of expertise.

Finally, the position to be taken – and the one that I will adopt here – could be that, however planned, purposeful actions are inevitably *situated actions*. By situated actions I mean simply actions taken in the context of particular, concrete circumstances. In this sense one could argue that we all act like the Trukese, however much some of us may talk like Europeans. We must act like the Trukese because the circumstances of our actions are never fully anticipated and are continuously changing around us. As a consequence our actions, while systematic, are never planned in the strong sense that cognitive science would have it. Rather, plans are best viewed as a weak resource for what is primarily *ad hoc* activity. It is only when we are pressed to account for the rationality of our actions, given the biases of European culture, that we invoke the guidance of a plan. Stated in advance, plans are necessarily vague, insofar as they must accommodate the unforeseeable contingencies of particular situations. Reconstructed in retrospect, plans systematically filter out precisely the particularity of detail that characterizes situated actions, in favor of those aspects of the actions that can be seen to accord with the plan.

This third implication, it seems, is not just a symmetric alternative to the other two, but is different in kind, and somewhat more serious. That is, it calls into question not just the adequacy of our distinctions along the dimensions of culture, kinds of activity, or degrees of expertise, but the very productivity of our starting premises – that representations of action such as plans could be the basis for an account of actions in particular situations. Because the third implication has to do with foundations, and not because there is no truth in the other two, I take the idea that actions are primarily situated, and that situated actions are essentially *ad hoc*, as the starting point for my investigations.

The view of action exemplified by the European navigator is now being reified in the design of intelligent machines. In this book I examine one such machine, as a way of uncovering the strengths and limitations of the general view that its design embodies. The view, that purposeful action is determined by plans, is deeply rooted in the Western human sciences as *the* correct model of the rational actor. The logical form of plans makes them attractive for the purpose of constructing a computational model of action, to the extent that for those fields devoted to what is now called cognitive science, the analysis and synthesis of plans effectively constitute the study of action. My own contention, however, is that as students of human action we ignore the Trukese navigator at our peril. While an account of how the European navigates may be in hand, the essential nature of action, however planned or unplanned, is situated. It behooves us, therefore, to study and to begin to find ways to describe the Trukese system.

There is an injunction in social studies of science to eschew interest in the validity of the products of science, in favor of an interest in their production. While I generally agree with this injunction, my investigation of one of the prevailing models of human action in cognitive science is admittedly and unabashedly interested. That is to say, I take it that there is a reality of human action, beyond either the cognitive scientist's models or my own accounts, to which both are trying to do justice. In that sense, I am not just examining the cognitive science model with the dispassion of the uncommitted anthropologist of science, I am examining it in light of an alternative account of human action to which I am committed, and which I attempt to clarify in the process.

Acknowledgements

The greatest single contribution to this project has been the combination of time, freedom to work, faith that something would come of it, and intellectual support provided by John Seely Brown, as manager of the Intelligent Systems Laboratory at Xerox Palo Alto Research Center. He and other colleagues have nourished my slowly developing appreciation for the "anthropologically strange" community comprising cognitive science and its related disciplines. In particular, I have benefited from discussions at PARC with Daniel Bobrow, Sarah Douglas, Richard Fikes, Austin Henderson, David Levy, Tom Moran, Jeff Shrager, Brian Smith, Kurt Vanlehn, and Terry Winograd, with Phil Agre and David Chapman of the Laboratory for Artificial Intelligence at MIT, and with Mark Weiser of the University of Maryland. Conversations and friendship with my PARC colleagues Randy Trigg (who has helped to get my thoughts on these matters unstuck on more than one occasion), Susan Newman, and Deborah Tatar have added continually to the development of these ideas, and I am grateful to Deborah as well for her editorial contributions to my writing. Finally, conversations with Stan Rosenschein of the Artificial Intelligence Center at SRI, on his idea of "situated automata," have opened yet another window for me onto the problem of how this community proposes that we understand action. Needless to say, while I am deeply grateful for the contribution of these colleagues to the strength of what follows, the weaknesses are of my own making.

In my own field of anthropology, I have enjoyed the intellectual companionship and personal friendship of Brigitte Jordan, whose creative energy and respectful sensibilities toward her own work and life are an example for mine. I am deeply grateful to Doug Macbeth, who guided my discovery of the field of social studies and its possibilities. While he would doubtless argue innumerable points in the pages that follow, his influence is there. James Heap, Michael Lynch, and Steve Woolgar each provided extensive and thoughtful responses to early drafts. Particularly in its early stages, this project benefited greatly from lively discussions at the Interaction Analysis Lab at Michigan State University, where Frederick Erickson, Richard Frankel, Brigitte Jordan, Willett Kempton, Bill Rittenberg, Ron Simons and others helped me first to penetrate the thickness of a video analysis. Jeanette Blomberg and, more recently, Julian Orr are anthropological colleagues in the PARC community, and I have enjoyed their company. Lisa Alfke of the PARC Technical Information Center has provided invaluable assistance and support in tracking down books and journal articles.

I am grateful to Hubert Dreyfus and John Gumperz, members of my dissertation committee at the University of California at Berkeley, for their substantive and stylistic contributions, and for their enthusiasm for the project. My dissertation advisor, Gerald Berreman, provides through his own career in anthropology an example of what ethical scholarship can be. While finding my work increasingly foreign and exotic, he has remained an unflagging supporter.

Finally, of course, I thank my friends new and old, in particular Mimi Montgomery, who, over the last ten years, along with these ideas, has been a constant companion.

1 Introduction

> The famous anthropological absorption with the (to us)
> exotic . . . is, thus, essentially a device for displacing
> the dulling sense of familiarity with which the
> mysteriousness of our own ability to relate perceptively
> to one another is concealed from us.
>
> (Geertz 1973, p. 14)

The problem of shared understanding, or mutual intelligibility, has
defined the field of social studies for the past hundred years. On
the one hand, interpreting the actions of others has been the social
scientist's task; to come up with accounts of the significance of
human actions is, after all, the principal charge of ethnographic
anthropology. On the other hand, to understand the mutual intelligibility of action as a mundane, practical accomplishment of members of the society is, in large measure, the social scientist's problem
or subject matter. An account of that accomplishment would constitute an account of the foundation of social order.

While studies of mutual intelligibility have been concerned exclusively with human action, we now have a technology that has
brought with it the idea that rather than just using machines, we
interact with them as well. Already, the notion of "human–
machine interaction" pervades both technical and popular discussion of computers, whether about their design or their use. In
the debate over specific problems in the design and use of interactive machines, however, no question is raised about the bases for
the very idea of human–machine interaction as such. And recent
developments in the social sciences regarding the foundations of

1

human interaction have had remarkably little influence on the discussion of interactive machines.

The following chapters examine the conception of purposeful action, and consequently of interaction, informing the design of interactive machines. My central concern in the investigation is a new manifestation of an old problem in the study of mutual intelligibility: namely, the relation between observable behavior and the processes, not available to direct observation, that make behavior meaningful. For psychological studies, the crucial processes are essentially cognitive, located inside the head of the actor, and include the formation and effect of beliefs, desires, intentions, and the like. For social studies, the crucial processes are interactional and circumstantial, located in the relationships among actors, and between actors and their embedding situations. In either case, the problem of meaningful action turns on the observation that behavior is inherently subject to indefinitely many ascriptions of meaning or intent, while meaning and intent are expressible through an indefinite number of possible behaviors. Whether the final arbiter of action's significance is taken to be private psychological processes, or accountability to the public world, the question to be resolved – what constitutes purposeful action and how is it understood – is the same.

The new manifestation of this question concerning the nature of purposeful action and its interpretation arises in research on machine intelligence. Theoretically, the goal of that research is a computational model of intelligent behavior that not only, given some input, produces the right output behavior, but that does so by simulating human cognitive processes. Practically, the goal is just a machine that, given some input, produces behavior that is useful and appropriate to the situation at hand. In either case, insofar as rightness or appropriateness of behavior means that behavior is accountably rational in the eyes of an other, the measure of success is at bottom an interactional one.

For the moment, at least, the question of theoretical versus practical criteria of adequacy for machine intelligence is rendered moot by the problems involved in constructing a device that even appears to behave in ways that are purposeful or intelligent, at least outside of the most highly constrained domains. It may simply turn out that the resistance of meaningful action to simulation in the absence of any deep understanding will defend us against false impressions of theoretical success. In any case, my purpose here is not to resolve the question of whether or not artificial intelligence is possible, but rather to clarify some existing troubles in the project of constructing intelligent, interactive machines, as a way of contributing to our understanding of human intelligence and interaction.

Every human tool relies upon, and reifies, some underlying conception of the activity that it is designed to support. As a consequence, one way to view the artifact is as a test on the limits of the underlying conception. In this book I examine an artifact built on a *planning model* of human action. The model treats a plan as something located in the actor's head, which directs his or her behavior. In contrast, I argue that artifacts built on the planning model confuse *plans* with *situated actions*, and recommend instead a view of plans as formulations of antecedent conditions and consequences of action that account for action in a plausible way. As ways of talking about action, plans as such neither determine the actual course of situated action nor adequately reconstruct it. While for purposes of practical action this limitation on plans is irrelevant, for purposes of a science of practical action it is crucial. Specifically, if we are interested in situated action itself, we need to look at how it is that actors use the resources that a particular occasion provides – including, but crucially not reducible to, formulations such as plans – to construct their action's developing purpose and intelligibility.

Beginning with a view of interaction, or communication – I shall use the two terms interchangeably – as the mutual intelligibility of action, I investigate the basis for beginning to speak of interaction between humans and machines. Chapter 2 introduces the notion of interactive artifacts, and its basis in certain properties of computing machines. Chapter 3 examines the view of plans as the basis for action and communication held by designers of artificially intelligent, interactive machines, while chapters 4 and 5 present the alternative view of action and communication as situated, drawn from recent developments in social science. Finally, chapters 6 and 7 offer an analysis of encounters between novice users of a machine and a computer-based system intended to be intelligent and interactive. The aim of the case study is not to criticize the particular design, but to view the design as reifying certain premises about purposeful action. The task is to articulate those premises, to see how they succeed as a basis for human–machine communication and how they fail, and to explore the implications of their success and failure both for the design of human–machine communication and for the general explication of purposeful action and mutual intelligibility.

2 Interactive artifacts

> Marginal objects, objects with no clear place, play im-
> portant roles. On the lines between categories, they
> draw attention to how we have drawn the lines. Some-
> times in doing so they incite us to reaffirm the lines,
> sometimes to call them into question, stimulating dif-
> ferent distinctions. (Turkle 1984, p. 31)

In *The Second Self* (1984), Sherry Turkle describes the computer as an
"evocative object," one that raises new questions regarding our
common sense of the distinction between artifacts and intelligent
others. Her studies include an examination of the impact of
computer-based artifacts on children's conceptions of the difference between categories such as "alive" versus "not alive," and
"machine" versus "person." In dealing with the questions that
computer-based objects evoke, children make clear that the dif-
ferentiation of physical from psychological entities, which as adults
we largely take for granted, is the end product of a process of establishing the relationship between the observable behavior of a thing
and its underlying nature.[1] Children have a tendency, for example,
to attribute life to physical objects on the basis of behavior such as
autonomous motion, or reactivity, though they reserve humanity
for entities evidencing such things as emotion, speech, and
apparent thought or purposefulness. Turkle's observation with
respect to computational artifacts is that children ascribe to them an
"almost aliveness," and a psychology, while maintaining their
distinctness from human beings: a view that, as Turkle points out,

[1] Though see Carey 1985, chapter 1 for a critique of the Piagetian notion that children
at first have no concept for mechanical causation apart from intentional causation.

is remarkable among other things for its correspondence to the views held by those who are the artifacts' designers.[2]

In this book I take as a point of departure a particular aspect of the phenomenon that Turkle identifies: namely, the apparent challenge that computational artifacts pose to the longstanding distinction between the physical and the social, in the special sense of those things that one designs, builds, and uses, on the one hand, and those things with which one communicates, on the other. While this distinction has been relatively non-problematic to date, now for the first time the term "interaction" – in a sense previously reserved for describing a uniquely interpersonal activity – seems appropriately to characterize what goes on between people and certain machines as well.[3] Interaction between people and machines implies mutual intelligibility, or shared understanding. What motivates my inquiry, therefore, is not only the recent question of how there could be mutual intelligibility between people and machines, but the prior question of how we account for the shared understanding, or mutual intelligibility, that we experience as people in our interactions with others whose essential sameness is not in question. An answer to the more recent question, theoretically at least, presupposes an answer to the earlier one.

In this chapter I relate the idea of human–machine communication to some distinctive properties of computational artifacts, and to the emergence of disciplines dedicated to making those artifacts

[2] See especially pp. 62–3; Turkle finds some cause for alarm in the fact that for children the distinction of machine and person seems to turn centrally on a separation of thought from feeling; that is, computers exhibit the former, but lack the latter. This view, she argues, includes a kind of dissociation of intellect and emotion, and consequent trivialization of both, that characterizes the attitudes of many in the field of Artificial Intelligence.

[3] Actually, the term "interaction" has its origins in the physical sciences, to describe a reciprocal action or influence. I use it here in the common sense assigned to it by social science: namely, to mean communication between persons. The migration of the term from the physical sciences to the social, and now back to some ground that stands between them, relates in intriguing ways to a general blurring of the distinction between physical and social in modern science, and to the general question of whether machines are actually becoming more like people or whether, in fact, people are coming to define themselves more as machines. There is clearly a mutual influence at work. For more on this last point, see Dreyfus 1979, ch. 9.

intelligent. I begin with a brief discussion of cognitive science, the interdisciplinary field devoted to modeling cognitive processes, and its role in the project of creating intelligent artifacts.[4] Along with a theoretical interest in intelligent artifacts, the computer's properties have inspired a practical effort at engineering interaction between people and machines. I argue that the description of computational artifacts as interactive is supported by their *reactive*, *linguistic*, and internally *opaque* properties. With those properties in mind, I consider the double sense in which researchers are interested in artifacts that explain themselves: on the one hand, as a solution to the longstanding problem of conveying the artifact's intended purpose to the user, through its design and attendant instructions and, on the other hand, as a means of establishing the intelligence, or rational accountability, of the artifact itself.

2.1 Automata and cognitive science

Historically the idea of *automata* – the possibility of constructing physical devices that are self-regulating in ways that we commonly associate with living, animate beings – has been closely tied to the simulation of animal forms. McCorduck (1979) points out that human-like automata have been constructed since Hellenic times: statues that moved, gestured, spoke, and generally were imbued by observers – even those well aware of the internal mechanisms that powered them – with everything from minds to souls.[5] In the fourteenth century in Western Europe, learned men were commonly believed to construct talking heads made of brass, considered as both the source of their creator's wisdom and its manifestation. More prosaically, Jacques de Vaucanson in the eighteenth century designed a series of renowned mechanical statues, the most famous being a duck, the inner workings of which produced a variety of simple outward behaviors.

---

[4] For an extensive treatment, see Gardner 1985.
[5] See McCorduck 1979, ch. 1; Churchland 1984, ch. 6. For a further history of automata, see Cohen 1966.

At the same time, Julien de la Mettrie published *Man, A Machine*, in which he argued that the vitality characteristic of human beings was the result of their physical *structure*, rather than either of something immanent in their material substance or of some immaterial force. Cognitive scientists today maintain the basic premise of de la Mettrie with respect to mind, contending that mind is best viewed as neither substantial nor insubstantial, but as an abstractable structure implementable in any number of possible physical substrates. Intelligence, in other words, is only incidentally embodied in the neurophysiology of the human brain, and what is essential about intelligence can be abstracted from that particular, albeit highly successful, substrate and embodied in an unknown range of alternative forms. This view decouples reasoning and intelligence from things uniquely human, and opens the way for the construction of intelligent artifacts.[6]

The preoccupation of cognitive science with mind in this abstract sense is in part a concern to restore meaning to psychological explanation (see Stich 1983, ch. 1). At the turn of this century, the recognized method for studying human mental life was introspection and, insofar as introspection was not amenable to the emerging canons of scientific method, the study of cognition seemed doomed to be irremediably unscientific. In reaction to that prospect, the behaviorists posited that all human action should be understandable in terms of publicly observable, mechanistically describable relations between the organism and its environment. In the name of turning cognitive studies into a science, in other words, the study of cognition as the study of something apart from overt behavior was effectively abandoned in mainstream psychology.

Cognitive science, in this respect, was a project to bring thought back into the study of human action, while preserving the commitment to scientism. Cognitive science reclaims mentalist constructs such as beliefs, desires, intentions, symbols, ideas, schemata, planning, and problem-solving. Once again human purposes are the

[6] See Turkle 1984, ch. 7; and McCorduck 1979, ch. 5. Turkle's description of the present academic AI culture at MIT is particularly insightful.

basis for cognitive psychology, but this time without the unconstrained speculation of the introspectionists. The study of cognition is to be empiricized not by a strict adherence to behaviorism, but by the use of a new technology: namely, the computer.

The sub-field of cognitive science most dedicated to the computer is artificial intelligence. Artificial intelligence arose as advances in computing technology were tied to developments in neurophysiological and mathematical theories of information. The requirement of computer modeling, of an "information processing psychology," seemed both to make theoretical sense and to provide the accountability that would make it possible to pursue a science of otherwise inaccessible mental phenomena. If a theory of underlying mental processes could be modeled on the computer so as to produce the right outward behavior, the theory could be viewed as having passed at least a sufficiency test of its psychological validity.

The cognitivist strategy is to interject a mental operation between environmental stimulus and behavioral response: in essence, to relocate the causes of action from the environment that impinges upon the actor to processes, abstractable as computation, in the actor's head. The first premise of cognitive science, therefore, is that people – or "cognizers" of any sort – act on the basis of symbolic representations: a kind of cognitive code, instantiated physically in the brain, on which operations are performed to produce mental states such as "the belief that *p*," which in turn produce behavior consistent with those states. The relation of environmental stimuli to those mental states, on the one hand, and of mental states to behavior, on the other, remains deeply problematic and widely debated within the field (see, for example, Fodor 1983; Pylyshyn 1974, 1984; Stich 1983). The agreement among all participants in cognitive science and its affiliated disciplines, however, is that cognition is not just potentially *like* computation, it literally *is* computational. There is no reason, in principle, why there should not be a computational account of mind, therefore, and there is no a priori reason to draw a principled boundary between people, taken as "information-processors" or "symbol manipulators" or, in

George Miller's phrase, "informavores" (Pylyshyn 1984, p. xi), and certain computing machines.

The view that intelligence is the manipulation of symbols finds practical implementation both in so-called expert systems, which structure and process large amounts of well-formulated data, and industrial robots that perform routine, repetitive assembly and control tasks. Expert systems – essentially sophisticated programs that manipulate data structures to accord with rules of inference that experts are understood to use – have minimal sensory-motor, or "peripheral," access to the world in which they are embedded, input being most commonly through a keyboard, by a human operator. Industrial robots – highly specialized, computer-controlled devices designed to perform autonomously a single repetitive physical task – have relatively more developed sensory–motor apparatus than do expert systems, but the success of robotics is still confined to specialized activities, under controlled conditions. In both cases, the systems can handle large amounts of encoded information, and syntactic relationships of great sophistication and complexity, in highly circumscribed domains. But when it comes either to direct interaction with the environment, or to the exercise of practical, everyday reasoning about the significance of events in the world, there is general agreement that the state-of-the-art in intelligent machines has yet to attain the basic cognitive abilities of the normal five-year-old child.

2.2 *The idea of human–computer interaction*

In spite of the current limits on machine intelligence, the use of an intentional vocabulary is already well established in both technical and popular discussion of computers. In part, the attribution of purpose to computer-based artifacts derives from the simple fact that each action by the user effects an immediate machine *reaction* (see Turkle 1984, ch. 8). The technical definition of "interactive computing" (see, for example, Oberquelle, Kupka, and Maass 1983, p. 313) is simply that real-time control over the computing process is placed in the hands of the user, through immediate processing and through the availability of interrupt facilities whereby the user can override and modify the operations in progress. This definition contrasts current capabilities with earlier forms of computing, specifically batch processing, where user commands were queued and executed without any intermediate feedback. The greater reactivity of current computers, combined with the fact that, like any machine, the computer's reactions are not random but by design, suggest the character of the computer as a purposeful, and, by association, as a social object.

A more profound basis for the relative sociability of computer-based artifacts, however, is the fact that the means for controlling computing machines and the behavior that results are increasingly *linguistic*, rather than mechanistic. That is to say, machine operation becomes less a matter of pushing buttons or pulling levers with some physical result, and more a matter of specifying operations and assessing their effects through the use of a common language.[7] With or without machine intelligence, this fact has contributed to the tendency of designers, in describing what goes on between people and machines, to employ terms borrowed from the description of human interaction – dialogue, conversation, and so forth: terms that carry a largely unarticulated collection of intuitions about properties common to human communication and the use of computer-based machines.

While for the most part the vocabulary of human interaction has been taken over by researchers in human–machine communication with little deliberation, several researchers have attempted to clarify similarities and differences between computer use and

---

[7] Notwithstanding the popular fantasy of the talking machine, the crucial element that invites a view of computers as interactive is language, not speech. While strictly speaking buttons and keys remain the principal input devices in computing, this is relatively trivial. The synthesis of speech by computers may well add to our inclination to ascribe understanding to them, but will not, in itself, contribute substantively to their sensibility. On the other hand, simulation of natural language understanding, even when the language is written rather than spoken, is proving to be a profoundly difficult problem that is inseparable from the problem of simulating intelligence as such.

human conversation. Perhaps the most thoughtful and comprehensive of these is Hayes and Reddy (1983). They identify the central difference between existing interactive computer systems and human communication as a question of "robustness," or the ability on the part of conversational participants to respond to unanticipated circumstances, and to detect and remedy troubles in communication:

> The ability to interact gracefully depends on a number of relatively independent skills: skills involved in parsing elliptical, fragmented, and otherwise ungrammatical input; in ensuring that communication is robust (ensuring that the intended meaning has been conveyed); in explaining abilities and limitations, actions and the motives behind them; in keeping track of the focus of attention of a dialogue; in identifying things from descriptions, even if ambiguous or unsatisfiable; and in describing things in terms appropriate for the context. While none of these components of graceful interaction has been entirely neglected in the literature, no single current system comes close to having most of the abilities and behaviours we describe, and many are not possessed by any current systems. (p. 232)

Hayes and Reddy believe, however, that:

> Even though there are currently no truly gracefully interacting systems, none of our proposed components of graceful interaction appears individually to be much beyond the current state of the art, at least for suitably restricted domains of discourse. (p. 232)

They then review the state of the art, including systems like LIFER (Hendrix 1977) and SCHOLAR (Carbonell 1971), which display sensitivity to the user's expectations regarding acknowledgement of input; systems that resolve ambiguity in English input from the user through questions (Hayes 1981); systems like the GUS system (Bobrow *et al.* 1977) which represent limited knowledge of the domain that the interaction is about; work on the maintenance of a common focus over the course of the interaction (Grosz 1977; Sidner 1979); and Hayes and Reddy's own work on an automated explanation facility in a simple service domain (1983).

Two caveats on Hayes and Reddy's prescription for a gracefully interacting system (both of which, to their credit, they freely admit) are worth noting. First, they view the abilities cited as necessary but not sufficient for human interaction, their claim for the list being simply that "it provides a good working basis from which to build gracefully interacting systems" (1983, p. 233). And, not surprisingly, the abilities that they cite constitute a list of precisely those problems currently under consideration in research on human–machine communication. There is, in other words, no independent assessment of how the problems on which researchers work relate to the nature and organization of human communication as such. Secondly, research on those problems that have been identified is confined to highly circumscribed domains. The consequence of working from an admittedly partial and *ad hoc* list of abilities, in limited domains, is that practical inroads in human–computer communication can be furthered, while the basic question of what human interaction comprises is deferred. Deferred as well is the question of why it is, beyond methodological convenience, that research in human–machine interaction has proceeded only in those limited domains that it has.

Moreover, while Hayes and Reddy take the position that "it is very important for a gracefully interacting system to conduct a dialogue in as human-like a way as possible" (ibid., p. 233), this assertion is a point of controversy in the research community. On the one side, there is an argument to the effect that one should acknowledge, and even exploit, the fact that people bring to computer use a tremendous range of skills and expectations from human interaction. Within research on human–computer interaction, for example, some progress has been made toward allowing people to enter commands into computers using natural language (i.e. languages like English, in contrast to programming languages). On the other side, even Hayes and Reddy admit that:

> the aim of being as human-like as possible must be tempered by the limited potential for comprehension of any foreseeable computer system. Until a solution is found to the problems of organizing and using the range of world knowledge possessed by a human, practical systems will only be able to comprehend a small amount of input, typically within a specific domain of expertise. Graceful interaction must, therefore, supplement its simulation of human conversational ability with strategies to deal naturally and gracefully with input that is not fully understood, and, if possible, to steer a conversation back to the system's home ground. (ibid., p. 233)

While Hayes and Reddy would make these recovery strategies invisible to the user, they also acknowledge the "habitability" problem identified by Watt (1968) with respect to language: that is, the tendency of human users to assume that a computer system has sophisticated linguistic abilities after it has displayed elementary ones. This tendency is not surprising, given the fact that our only precedent for language-using entities to date has been other human beings. As soon as computational artifacts demonstrate *some* evidence of recognizably human abilities, we are inclined to endow them with the rest. The misconceptions that ensue, however, lead some like Fitter (1979) to argue that English or other "natural" languages are in fact not natural for purposes of human–computer interaction:

> for the purpose of man–computer communication, *a natural language is one that makes explicit the knowledge and processes for which the man and computer share a common understanding* . . . it becomes the responsibility of the systems designer to provide a language structure which will make apparent to the user the procedures on which it is based and will not lead

him to expect from the computer unrealistic powers of inference. (ibid., p. 340, original emphasis)

In view of our tendency to ascribe full intelligence on the basis of partial evidence, the recommendation is that designers might do best to make available to the user the ways in which the system is *not* like a participant in interaction.[8] In this spirit, Nickerson (1976) argues that:

The model that seems appropriate for this view of person–computer interaction is that of an individual making use of a sophisticated tool and not that of one person conversing with another. The term "user" is, of course, often used to denote the human component in a person–computer interaction, as it has been in this paper. It is, to my taste, preferable to the term "partner," not only because it seems more descriptive of the nature of the relationships that existing systems permit, and that future systems are likely to, but because it implies an asymmetry with respect to goals and objectives that "partner" does not. "User" is not a term that one would normally apply to a participant in a conversation. (p. 111)

The argument that computational processes should be revealed to the user, however, is potentially counter to the promotion of an intentional vocabulary in speaking about computer-based devices. As Dennett (1978) points out, it is in part our inability to see inside each other's heads, or our mutual *opacity*, that makes intentional explanations so powerful in the interpretation of human action. So it is in part the internal complexity and opacity of the computer that invites an intentional stance. This is the case not only because users lack technical knowledge of the computer's internal workings but because, even for those who possess such knowledge, there is an

---

[8] In fact, Nickerson (1976) points out that there are some ways in which a computer is not like another person which lend a certain advantage to the user, e.g. interruptions can be made without concern about giving offense, responses can be delayed as long as is necessary.

"irreducibility" to the computer as an object that is unique among human artifacts (Turkle 1984, p. 272). The overall behavior of the computer is not describable, that is to say, with reference to any of the simple local events that it comprises; it is precisely the behavior of a myriad of those events in combination that constitutes the overall machine. To refer to the behavior of the machine, then, one must speak of "its" functionality. And once reified as an entity, the inclination to ascribe actions to the entity rather than to the parts is irresistible.

Intentional explanations relieve us of the burden of understanding mechanism, insofar as one need assume only that the design is rational in order to call upon the full power of common-sense psychology and have, ready at hand, a basis for anticipating and construing an artifact's behavior. At the same time, precisely because the mechanism is in fact unknown, and, insofar as underspecification is taken to be characteristic of human beings (as evidenced by the fact that we are inclined to view something that is fully specified as less than human), the personification of the machine is reinforced by the ways in which its inner workings are a mystery, and its behavior at times surprises us. Insofar as the machine is somewhat predictable, in sum, and yet is also both internally opaque and liable to unanticipated behavior, we are more likely to view ourselves as engaged in interaction with it than as just performing operations upon it, or using it as a tool to perform operations upon the world (see MacKay 1962).

2.3 Self-explanatory artifacts

In the preceding pages I have proposed that the reactive, linguistic, and opaque properties of the computer lead us to view it as interactive, and to apply intentional explanations to its behavior. This tie to intentionality has both theoretical and practical implications. Practically, it suggests that, like a human actor, the computer should be able to explain itself, or the intent behind its actions, to the user. Theoretically, it suggests that the computer actually has intent, as demonstrated precisely in this ability to behave in an accountably rational, intelligible way.

For practical purposes, "user interface" designers[9] have long held the view that machines ideally should be self-explanatory, in the broad sense that their operation should be discoverable without extensive training, from information provided on or through the machine itself. On this view, the degree to which an artifact is self-explanatory is just the extent to which someone examining the artifact is able to reconstruct the *designer's intentions* regarding its use. This basic idea, that a self-explanatory artifact is one whose intended purpose is discoverable by the user, is presumably as old as the design and use of tools. With respect to computer-based artifacts, however, the notion of a self-explanatory artifact has taken on a second sense: namely, the idea that the artifact might actually *explain itself* in something more like the sense that a human being does. In this second sense the goal is that the artifact should not only be intelligible to the user as a tool, but that it should be *intelligent* – that is, able to understand the actions of the user, and to provide for the rationality of its own.

In the remainder of this chapter, I look at these two senses of a self-explanatory machine and at the relation between them. The first sense – that a tool should be decipherable by its user – reflects the fact that artifacts are constructed by designers, for a purpose, and that the user of a tool needs to know something of that design intent. Given their interactional properties, computational tools seem to offer unique capabilities for the provision of instruction to their users. The idea that instructions could be presented more effectively using the power of computation is not far from the idea that computer-based artifacts could actually instruct: that is, could interact with people in a way that approximates the behavior of an intelligent human expert or coach. And this second idea, that the

---

[9] In design parlance, the term "user interface" refers both to the physical place at which the user issues commands to a device, finds reports of its state, or obtains the products of its operation, and the procedures by which those interactions occur.

artifact could actually interact instructively with the user, ties the practical problem of instruction to the theoretical problem of building an intelligent, interactive machine.

2.3.1 *The computer as an artifact designed for a purpose*
At the same time that computational artifacts introduce new complexity and opacity into our encounters with machines, our reliance on computer-based technology and its proliferation throughout the society increases. One result is the somewhat paradoxical objective that increasingly complex technology should be usable with decreasing amounts of training. Rather than relying upon the teachings of an experienced user, the use of computers is to be conveyed directly through the technology itself.

The inherent difficulty of conveying the use of a technology directly through its design is well known to archaeologists, who have learned that while the attribution of design intent is a requirement for an artifact's intelligibility, the artifact's design as such does not convey unequivocally either its actual or its intended use. While this problem in construing the purpose of artifacts can be alleviated, it can never fully be resolved, and it defines the essential problem that the novice user of the tool confronts. Insofar as the goal of a tool's design is that use of the tool should be self-evident, therefore, the problem of deciphering an artifact defines the problem of the designer as well.

As with any communication, instructions for the use of a tool are constrained by the general maxim that utterances should be designed for their recipients. The extent to which the maxim is observed is limited in the first instance by the resources that the medium of communication affords. Face-to-face human interaction is the paradigm case of a system for communication that, because it is organized for maximum context-sensitivity, supports a response designed for just these recipients, on just this occasion. Face-to-face instruction brings that context-sensitivity to bear on problems of skill acquisition. The gifted coach, for example, draws on powers of language and observation, and uses the situation of instruction, in order to specialize instruction for the individual student. Where written instruction relies upon generalizations about its recipient and the occasion of its use, the coach draws pedagogical strength from exploitation of the unique details of particular situations.[10]

A consequence of the human coach's method is that his or her skills must be deployed anew each time. An instruction manual, in contrast, has the advantage of being durable, re-usable, and replicable. In part, the strength of written text is that, in direct contrast to the pointed commentary of the coach, text allows the *disassociation* of the occasion of an instruction's production from the occasion of its use. For the same reason, however, text affords relatively poor resources for recipient design. The promise of interactive computer systems, in these terms, is a technology that can move instructional design away from the written manual in the direction of the human coach, and the resources afforded by face-to-face interaction.

Efforts at building self-explicating machines in their more sophisticated forms now adopt the metaphor of the machine as an expert, and the user as a novice, or student. Among the most interesting attempts to design such a computer-based "coach" is a system called WEST (Burton and Brown 1982). The design strategy adopted in WEST is based on the observation that the skill of a human coach lies as much in what isn't said as what is. Specifically, the human coach does not disrupt the student's engagement in an activity in order to ask questions, but instead diagnoses a student's strengths and weaknesses through observation. And once the

---

[10] Face-to-face interaction is in most cases a necessary, but of course never a sufficient, condition for successful human coaching. Coombs and Alty (1984) provide an interesting discussion of the failings of interactions between human advisors and new computer users. At the same time, they point out that the characteristics of the advisory sessions that new users found unsatisfactory show marked similarities to human interactions with most rule-based computer help systems, e.g. that the advisors provide only the recommended solutions to reported problems, while failing either to elicit the view of the user, or to articulate any of their own rationale. Satisfactory sessions, in contrast, were characterized by what initially appeared to be less structure and less economy, but which on further investigation was revealed as "well-motivated despite surface appearances, the objective not being strict problem-solving as we had assumed, but problem-solving through mutual understanding. This required sensitivity to different structural factors" (pp. 24–5).

diagnosis is made, the coach interjects advice and instruction selectively, in ways designed to maximize learning through discovery and experience. In that spirit, the WEST system attempts to infer the student's knowledge of the domain – in this case a computer game called "How the West was Won," designed to teach the use of basic arithmetic expressions – by observing the student's behavior.[11]

While the project of identifying a student's problems directly from his or her behavior proved considerably more difficult than expected, the objectives for the WEST coach were accomplished in the prototype system to an impressive degree. Because in the case of learning to play WEST the student's actions take the form of input to the computer (entries on a keyboard) and therefore leave an accessible trace, and because a context for those actions (the current state of, and history of consecutive moves across, the "board") is defined by the system, each student turn can be compared against calculations of the move that a hypothetical expert player would make given the same conditions. Each expert move, in turn, requires a stipulated set of associated skills. Evidence that a particular skill is lacking, accumulated across some number of moves, identifies that skill as a candidate for coaching. The coach then interjects offers of advice to the student at opportune moments in

---

[11] The student is presented with a graphic display of a game board made up of 70 squares (representing the Western frontier), a pair of icons (representing the two players – user and computer), and three spinners. A player's task in each turn is to combine the three numbers that the spinners provide, using the basic operations, to produce a value that becomes the number of spaces the icon is moved along the board. To add an element of strategy, squares on the board are more and less desirable – for example, "towns" occur every ten spaces, and landing on one advances you to the next. The object is to be the first player to land on 70.

Early observation of students playing the game revealed that they were not gaining the full benefit of the arithmetic practice, in that they tended to settle on a method for combining numbers (for example, multiply the first two numbers and add the third), and to repeat that same methods at each turn. Recognizing that this might reflect either a weakness in the student's proficiency at constructing expressions, a failure to grasp the strategy of the game, or both, Brown and Burton saw the potential usefulness of a "coach" that could guide the student to an expanded repertoire of skills and a better understanding of the domain. For a description of a similarly motivated "advisory" system for the programming language PROLOG, see Coombs and Alty 1984.

the course of the play, where what constitutes an opportune moment for interjection is determined according to a set of rules of thumb regarding good tutorial strategy (for example, always coach by offering the student an alternative move that both demonstrates the relevant skill and accomplishes obviously superior results; never coach on two turns in a row, no matter what, and so forth).

2.3.2 *The computer as an artifact having purposes*

While the computer-based coach can be understood as a logical development in the longstanding problem of instruction, the requirement that it be interactive introduces a second sense of self-explanatory machine which is more recent, and is uniquely tied to the advent of computing. The new idea is that the intelligibility of artifacts is not just a matter of the availability to the user of the *designer's* intentions for the artifact, but of the intentions of the *artifact* itself. That is to say, the designer's objective now is to imbue the machine with the grounds for behaving in ways that are accountably rational: that is, reasonable or intelligible to others, including, in the case of interaction, ways that are responsive to the other's actions.

In 1950, A. M. Turing proposed a now-famous, and still controversial, test for machine intelligence based on a view of intelligence as accountable rationality. Turing argued that if a machine could be made to respond to questions in such a way that a person asking the questions could not distinguish between the machine and another human being, the machine would have to be described as intelligent. To implement his test, Turing chose a game called the "imitation game." The game was initially conceived as a test of the ability of an interrogator to distinguish which of two respondents was a man and which a woman. To eliminate the evidence of physical embodiment, the interaction was to be conducted remotely, via a teleprinter. Thus Turing's notion that the game could easily be adapted to a test of machine intelligence, by substituting the machine for one of the two human respondents.

Turing expressly dismissed as a possible objection to his

21

proposed test the contention that, although the machine might succeed in the game, it could succeed through means that bear no resemblance to human thought. Turing's contention was precisely that success at performing the game, regardless of mechanism, is sufficient evidence for intelligence (Turing 1950, p. 435). The Turing test thereby became the canonical form of the argument that if two information-processors, subject to the same input stimuli, produce indistinguishable output behavior, then, regardless of the identity of their internal operations, one processor is essentially equivalent to the other.

The lines of the controversy raised by the Turing test were drawn over a family of programs developed by Joseph Weizenbaum in the 1960s under the name ELIZA, designed to support "natural language conversation" with a computer (Weizenbaum 1983, p. 23). Of the name ELIZA, Wiezenbaum writes:

> Its name was chosen to emphasize that it may be incremen-
> tally improved by its users, since its language abilities may
> be continually improved by a "teacher." Like the Eliza of
> *Pygmalion* fame, it can be made to appear even more civil-
> ized, the relation of appearance to reality, however, remain-
> ing in the domain of the playwright. (p. 23)

Anecdotal reports of occasions on which people approached the teletype to one of the ELIZA programs and, believing it to be connected to a colleague, engaged in some amount of "interaction" without detecting the true nature of their respondent, led many to believe that Weizenbaum's program had passed a simple form of the Turing test. Notwithstanding its apparent interactional success, however, Weizenbaum himself denied the intelligence of the program, on the basis of the underlying mechanism which he described as "a mere collection of procedures" (p. 23):

> The gross procedure of the program is quite simple; the text
> [written by the human participant] is read and inspected for
> the presence of a *keyword*. If such a word is found, the sen-

tence is transformed according to a *rule* associated with the keyword, if not a content-free remark or, under certain conditions, an earlier transformation is retrieved. The text so computed or retrieved is then printed out. (p. 24, original emphasis)

In spite of Weizenbaum's disclaimers with respect to their intelligence, the ELIZA programs are still cited as instances of successful interaction between human and machine. The grounds for their success are clearest in DOCTOR, one of the ELIZA programs whose script equipped it to respond to the human user as if the computer were a Rogerian therapist and the user a patient. The DOCTOR program exploited the maxim that shared premises can remain unspoken: that the less we say in conversation, the more what is said is assumed to be self-evident in its meaning and implications (see Coulter 1979, ch. 5). Conversely, the very fact that a comment is made without elaboration implies that such shared background assumptions exist. The more elaboration or justification is provided, the less the appearance of transparence or self-evidence. The less elaboration there is, the more the recipient will take it that the meaning of what is provided should be obvious.

The design of the DOCTOR program, in other words, exploited the natural inclination of people to deploy what Karl Mannheim first termed the *documentary method of interpretation* to find the sense of actions that are assumed to be purposeful or meaningful (Garfinkel 1967, p. 78). Very simply, the documentary method refers to the observation that people take appearances as evidence for, or the document of, an ascribed underlying reality, while taking the reality so ascribed as a resource for the interpretation of the appearance. In the case of DOCTOR, computer-generated responses that might otherwise seem odd were rationalized by users on the grounds that there must be some psychiatric intent behind them, not immediately obvious to the user as "patient," but sensible nonetheless:

If, for example, one were to tell a psychiatrist "I went for a long boat ride" and he responded "Tell me about boats," one would not assume that he knew nothing about boats, but that he had some purpose in so directing the subsequent conversation. It is important to note that this assumption is one made by the speaker. Whether it is realistic or not is an altogether different question. In any case, it has a crucial psychological utility in that it serves the speaker to maintain his sense of being heard and understood. The speaker further defends his impression (which even in real life may be illusory) by attributing to his conversational partner all sorts of background knowledge, insights and reasoning ability. But again, these are the speaker's contribution to the conversation. They manifest themselves inferentially in the *interpretations* he makes of the offered response. (Weizenbaum 1983, p. 26, original emphasis)

In explicating the ELIZA programs, Weizenbaum was primarily concerned with the inclination of human users to find sense in the computer's output, and to ascribe to it an understanding, and therefore an authority, unwarranted by the actual mechanism.[12] While unmasking the intelligence of his program, however, Weizenbaum continued to describe it as "a program which makes

---

[12] In this regard it is interesting to note that a great debate ensued surrounding the status of the DOCTOR program as a psychotherapeutic tool. That debate took on a humorous tone when Weizenbaum submitted a letter to the Forum of the Association for Computing Machinery, an excerpt from which follows:

Below is a listing of a PL/1 program that causes a typewriter console to imitate the verbal behavior of an autistic patient. The "doctor" types his interrogatories on the console. It responds exactly as does an autistic patient – that is, not at all. I have validated this model following the procedure first used in commercial advertising by Carter's Little Liver Pills ("Seven New York doctors say . . .") and later used so brilliantly by Dr K. M. Colby in his simulation of paranoia [a reference to Colby. K. M. *et al.* 1972]; I gave N psychiatrists access to my program and asked each to say from what mental disorder it suffered. M psychiatrists (M<N) said the (expletive deleted) program was autistic. (The methodological assumption here is that if two processes have identical input/output behaviors, then one constitutes an explanation of the other.)

The program has the advantage that it can be implemented on a plain typewriter not connected to a computer at all. (Weizenbaum 1983, p. 28)

natural language conversation with a computer possible" (1983, p. 23). Nevertheless, as part of his disclaimer regarding its intelligence, Weizenbaum points to a crucial shortcoming in the ELIZA strategy with respect to conversation:

> ELIZA in its use so far has had as one of its principal objectives the concealment of its lack of understanding. But to encourage its conversational partner to offer inputs from which it can select remedial information, it must *reveal* its misunderstanding. A switch of objectives from the concealment to the revelation of misunderstanding is seen as a precondition to making an ELIZA-like program the basis for an effective natural language man–machine communication system. (p. 27, original emphasis)

More recently, the inevitability of troubles in communication, and the importance of their remedy to the accomplishment of "graceful interaction," has been re-introduced into the human–machine communication effort by Hayes and Reddy (1983). They observe that:

> During the course of a conversation, it is not uncommon for people to misunderstand or fail to understand each other. Such failures in communication do not usually cause the conversation to break down; rather, the participants are able to resolve the difficulty, usually by a short clarifying sub-dialogue, and continue with the conversation from where they left off. Current computer systems are unable to take part in such clarifying dialogues, or resolve communication difficulties in any other way. As a result, when such difficulties occur, a computer dialogue system is unable to keep up its end of the conversation, and a complete breakdown is likely to result; this fragility lies in stark and unfavourable contrast to the robustness of human dialogue. (p. 234)

Hayes and Reddy go on to recommend steps toward a remedy for the fragility of human–computer interaction, based on the incorporation, from human communication, of conventions for the detection and repair of misunderstanding. They acknowledge, however, that their recommendations are unlikely to be sufficient for successful communication in other than the simplest encounters, e.g. automated directory assistance, or reservation systems. The question of why this should be so – of the nature of the limits on human–machine communication, and the nature and extent of robustness in human interaction – is the subject of the following chapters.

3 *Plans*

> Once the European navigator has developed his
> operating plan and has available the appropriate tech-
> nical resources, the implementation and monitoring of
> his navigation can be accomplished with a minimum of
> thought. He has simply to perform almost mechani-
> cally the steps dictated by his training and by his initial
> planning synthesis. (Gladwin 1964, p. 175)

Every account of communication involves assumptions about
action, in particular about the bases for action's coherence and intelligibility. This chapter and the next discuss two alternative views of
action. The first, adopted by most researchers in artificial intelligence, locates the organization and significance of human action in
underlying plans. As old at least as the Occidental hills, this view of
purposeful action is the basis for traditional philosophies of rational
action and for much of the behavioral sciences. It is hardly surprising, therefore, that it should be embraced by those newer fields
concerned with intelligent artifacts, particularly cognitive science
and information-processing psychology.

On the planning view, plans are prerequisite to and prescribe
action, at every level of detail. Mutual intelligibility is a matter of
the reciprocal recognizability of our plans, enabled by common conventions for the expression of intent, and shared knowledge about
typical situations and appropriate actions. The alternative view, developed here in chapter 4, is that while the course of action can
always be projected or reconstructed in terms of prior intentions
and typical situations, the prescriptive significance of intentions for
situated action is inherently vague. The coherence of situated

action is tied in essential ways not to individual predispositions or conventional rules but to local interactions contingent on the actor's particular circumstances. A consequence of action's situated nature is that communication must incorporate both a sensitivity to local circumstances and resources for the remedy of troubles in understanding that inevitably arise.

This chapter reviews the planning model of purposeful action and shared understanding. Those who adopt the planning model as a basis for interaction between people and machines draw on three related theories about the mutual intelligibility of action: (1) the planning model itself, which takes the significance of action to be derived from plans, and identifies the problem for interaction as their recognition and coordination, (2) speech act theory, which accounts for the recognizability of plans or intentions by proposing conventional rules for their expression, and (3) the idea of shared background knowledge, as the common resource that stands behind individual action and gives it social meaning. Each of these theories promises to solve general problems in human communication, such as the relation of observable behavior to intent, the correspondence of intended and interpreted meaning, and the stability of meaning assignments across situations, in ways that are relevant to particular problems in people's interaction with machines.

3.1 *The planning model*

The planning model in cognitive science treats a plan as a sequence of actions designed to accomplish some preconceived end. The model posits that action is a form of problem solving, where the actor's problem is to find a path from some initial state to a desired goal state, given certain conditions along the way.[1] Actions are described, at whatever level of detail, by their preconditions and their consequences:

---

[1] See Newell and Simon 1972 for the seminal formulation of this view.

In problem-solving systems, actions are described by pre-requisites (i.e. what must be true to enable the action), effects (what must be true after the action has occurred), and decomposition (how the action is performed, which is typically a sequence of subactions). (Allen 1984, p. 126)

Goals define the actor's relationship to the situation of action, since the situation is just those conditions that obstruct or advance the actor's progress toward his or her goals. Advance planning is inversely related to prior knowledge of the environment of action, and of the conditions that the environment is likely to present. Unanticipated conditions will require re-planning. In every case, however, whether constructed entirely in advance, or completed and modified during the action's course, the plan is prerequisite to the action.

3.1.1 *Plan generation and execution monitoring*
One of the earliest attempts to implement the planning model on a machine occurred as part of a project at Stanford Research Institute, beginning in the mid 1960s. The project's goal was to build a robot that could navigate autonomously through a series of rooms, avoiding obstacles and moving specified objects from one room to another. The robot, named by its designers Shakey, was controlled by a problem-solving program called STRIPS, which employed a means–end analysis to determine the robot's path (Fikes and Nilsson 1971). The STRIPS program examined the stated goal, and then determined a subset of operators, or actions available to the robot that would produce that state. The preconditions of those actions in turn identified particular subgoal states, which could be examined in the same way. The system thus worked backward from the goal until a plan was defined from the initial state to the goal state, made up of actions that the robot could perform. Subsequent work on problem solving and plan synthesis consisted in large part in refinements to this basic means–ends strategy, toward the end of achieving greater efficiency by constraining the search through possible solution paths.[2]

[2] For a review of subsequent work, see Sacerdoti 1977, ch. 3.

Beyond the problem of constructing plans, artificial intelligence researchers have had to address problems of what Nilsson (1973) terms "failure and surprise" in the execution of their planning programs, due to the practical exigencies of action in an unpredictable environment. The objective that Shakey should actually be able to move autonomously through a real (albeit somewhat impoverished) environment added a new class of problems to those faced by mathematical or game-playing programs operating in an abstract formal domain:

> for a problem-solver in a formal domain is essentially done when it has constructed a plan for a solution; nothing can go wrong. A robot in the real world, however, must consider the execution of the plan as a major part of every task. Unexpected occurrences are not unusual, so that the use of sensory feedback and corrective action are crucial. (Raphael, cited in McCorduck 1979, p. 224)

In Shakey's case, execution of the plan generated by the STRIPS program was monitored by a program called PLANEX. The PLANEX program monitored not the actual moves of the robot, however, but the execution of the plan. The program simply assumed that the execution of the plan meant that the robot had taken the corresponding action in the real world. The program also made the assumption that every time the robot moved there was some normally distributed margin of error that would be added to a "model of the world," or representation of the robot's location. When the cumulative error in the representation got large enough, the plan monitor initiated another part of the program that triggered a camera which could, in turn, take a reading of Shakey's location in the actual world.

The uncertainty to which Shakey was to respond consisted in changes made to the objects in its environment. Another order of uncertainty was introduced with Sacerdoti's system NOAH (an acronym for Nets of Action Hierarchies). Also developed at the

Stanford Research Institute as part of the Computer-Based Consultant project, NOAH was designed to monitor and respond to the actions of a human user. With NOAH, Sacerdoti extended the techniques of problem-solving and execution monitoring developed in the planning domain to the problem of interactive instruction:

> NOAH is an integrated problem solving and execution monitoring system. Its major goal is to provide a framework for storing expertise about the actions of a particular task domain, and to impart that expertise to a human in the cooperative achievement of nontrivial tasks. (Sacerdoti 1977, p. 2)

The output of the planning portion of Sacerdoti's program is a "procedural net," or hierarchy of partially ordered actions, which becomes in turn the input to the execution-monitoring portion of the system. The execution monitor takes the topmost action in the hierarchy, provides the user with an instruction, and then queries the user regarding the action's completion. A principal objective of the innovations that Sacerdoti introduced for the representation of procedures in NOAH was to extend execution monitoring to include tracking and assessment of the user's actions in response to the instructions generated:

> The system will monitor the apprentice's work to ensure that the operation is proceeding normally. When the system becomes aware of an unexpected event, it will alter instructions to the apprentice to deal effectively with the new situation. (ibid., p. 3)

A positive response from the user to the system's query regarding the action is taken to mean that the user understood the instruction, and has successfully carried it out, while a negative response is taken as a request for a more detailed instruction. The system allows as well for a "motivation response," or query from the user as to why a certain task needs to be done (to which the system responds by listing tasks to which the current task is related), and for an "error response," or indication from the user that the current instruction cannot be carried out.

Just as the accumulation of error in the PLANEX program required feedback from the world in order to re-establish the robot's location, the error response from the user in Sacerdoti's system requires that NOAH somehow repair its representation of the user's situation:

> PLANEX presumed that an adequate mechanism existed for accurately updating the world model. This was almost the case, since there were only a small number of actions that the robot vehicle could take, and the model of each action contained information about the uncertainty it would introduce in the world model. When uncertainties reached a threshold, the vision subsystem was used to restore the accuracy of the world model.
>
> For the domain of the Computer-based Consultant, or even for a richer robot domain, this approach will prove inadequate ... NOAH cannot treat the world model as a given. It must initiate interactions with the user at appropriate points to ensure that it is accurately monitoring the course of the execution ...
>
> [W]hen a serious error is discovered (requiring the system to be more thorough in its efforts to determine the state of the world), the system must determine what portions of its world model differ from the actual situation. (ibid., pp. 71–2)

The situation in which Shakey moved consisted of walls and boxes (albeit boxes that could be moved unexpectedly by a human hand). The problem in designing Shakey was to maintain consistency between the represented environment and the physical environment in which the robot moved. In introducing the actions of a user, the computer's environment becomes not only a physical but a social one, requiring the interpretation of the user's actions, and an assessment of the user's understanding of his or her situation. The difficulty of maintaining a shared understanding of a situation, as we will see more clearly in chapters 4 and 5, is not just a matter of monitoring the course of events, but of establishing their significance. Nonetheless, with Sacerdoti we have at least a preliminary recognition of the place of the situation in the intelligibility of action and communication.

3.1.2 *Interaction and plan recognition*

Adherents of the planning model in artificial intelligence research have taken the requirement of interaction as an injunction to extend the planning model from a single individual to two or more individuals acting in concert. The planning model attempts to bring concerted action under the jurisdiction of the individual actor by attaching to the others in the actor's world sufficient description, and granting to the actor sufficient knowledge, that he or she is able to respond to the actions of others as just another set of environmental conditions. The problem of social interaction, consequently, becomes an extension of the problem of the individual actor. The basic view of a single, goal-directed agent, acting in response to an environment of conditions, is complicated – the conditions now include the actions of other agents – but intact.

The problem for interaction, on this view, is to recognize the actions of others as the expression of their underlying plans. The complement to plan generation and execution in artificial intelligence research, therefore, is plan recognition, or the attribution of plans to others based on observation of their actions. The starting premise for a theory of plan recognition is that an observer takes some sequence of actions as evidence, and then forms hypotheses about the plans that could motivate and explain those actions. One persisting difficulty for action understanding in artificial intelligence research has been the uncertain relation between actions and intended effects. Allen (1984) illustrates this problem with the example of turning on a light:

> There are few physical activities that are a necessary part of performing the action of turning on a light. Depending on the context, vastly different patterns of behavior can be

classified as the same action. For example, turning on a light usually involves flipping a light switch, but in some circumstances it may involve tightening the light bulb (in the basement) or hitting the wall (in an old house). Although we have knowledge about how the action can be performed, this does not define what the action is. The key defining characteristic of turning on the light seems to be that the agent is performing some activity which will cause the light, which was off when the action started, to become on when the action ends. An important side effect of this definition is that we could recognize an observed pattern of activity as "turning on the light" even if we had never seen or thought about that pattern previously. (p. 126)

Allen's point is two-fold. First, the "same" action as a matter of intended effect can be achieved in any number of ways, where the ways are contingent on circumstance rather than on definitional properties of the action. And secondly, while an action can be accounted for *post hoc* with reference to its intended effect, an action's course cannot be predicted from knowledge of the actor's intent, nor can the course be inferred from observation of the outcome. Allen identifies the indeterminate relationship of intended effect to method as a problem for planning or plan recognition systems: a problem that he attempts to resolve by constructing a logical language for action descriptions that handles the distinction between what he calls the "causal definition" of an action (i.e. the pre and post conditions that must hold in order to say that the action has occurred, independent of any method), and the action's characterization in terms of a particular method or procedure for its accomplishment.[3]

---

[3] Another, less problematic uncertainty that Allen attempts to capture is the observation that while some components of an action are sequentially ordered in a necessary way (i.e. one is prerequisite to the other), other components, while necessary to the action, have no necessary sequential relationship to each other. The incorporation of unordered actions into the structure of plans, pioneered by Sacerdoti (1975), was viewed as a substantial breakthrough in early planning research.

While Allen's approach to the problem of plan recognition is an attempt to reconstruct logically our vocabulary of purposeful action, a few more psychologically oriented researchers in artificial intelligence have undertaken experiments designed to reveal the process by which people bring the actions of others under the jurisdiction of an ascribed plan. Schmidt, Sridharan, and Goodson (1978) observe, for example, that plan attribution seems to require certain transformations of the sequential organization of the action described.[4] They report that throughout the process of plan attribution the problem to be solved by the subject remains "ill-formed," by which they mean that at any given time neither the range of possible plans that the other might be carrying out, nor the criteria for assessing just what plan is actually in effect, are clearly defined (p. 80). Nonetheless, they report that their subjects are able to posit an underlying plan. Their strategy appears to be to adopt tentatively a single hypothesis about the other's plan, rather than entertain all or even some number of logical possibilities simultaneously. The preferred hypothesis regarding the other's plan then affects what actions are noted and recalled in the subject's accounts of the action, and the temporal order of events is restructured into logical "in order to" or "because" relationships, such that relations among actions are not restricted to consecutive events in time. At the same time, the current hypothesis is always subject to elaboration or revision in light of subsequent events, to the extent that subjects are often required to suspend judgment on a given hypothesis, and to adopt a "wait and see" strategy. Wherever possible, actions that violate the structure of an attributed plan are explained away before the plan itself is reconsidered. Schmidt, Shridharan, and Goodson conclude that all of these observations "support the generalization that action understanding is simply a process of plan recognition" (p. 50). It is worth noting, however, that while these observations clearly point to a

---

[4] The empiricism of their study is unusual in artificial intelligence research, where work generally proceeds on the basis of imagination and introspection.

process of plan attribution by the observer, there is no independent evidence that the process of plan attribution is a process of recognizing the plan of the actor.

3.1.3 *The status of plans*

Assessment of the planning model is complicated by equivocation in the literature between plans as a conceptual framework for the analysis and simulation of action, and plans as a psychological mechanism for its actual production. When researchers describe human action in terms of plans, the discussion generally finesses the question of just how the formulations provided by the researcher are purported to relate to the actor's intent. The claim is at least that people analyze each other's actions into goals and plans in order to understand each other. But the suggestion that the plan is "recognized" implies that it has an existence prior to and independent of the attribution: that it actually determines the action.

The identification of the plan with the actor's intent is explicit in the writing of philosophers of action supportive of artificial intelligence research, like Margaret Boden, who writes:

> unless an intention is thought of as an action-plan that can draw upon background knowledge and utilize it in the guidance of behavior one cannot understand how intentions function in real life. (1973, pp. 27–8)

Intentions, in other words are realized as plans-for-action that directly guide behavior. A logical extension of Boden's view, particularly given an interest in rendering it more computable, is the view that plans actually are prescriptions or instructions for action. An early and seminal articulation of this view came from Miller, Galanter, and Pribram (1960), who define an intention as "the uncompleted parts of a Plan whose execution has already begun" (p. 61). With respect to the plan itself:

> Any complete description of behavior should be adequate to

serve as a set of instructions, that is, it should have the characteristics of a plan that could guide the action described. When we speak of a plan ... the term will refer to a *hierarchy* of instructions ... *A plan is any hierarchical process in the organism that can control the order in which a sequence of operations is to be performed.*

A Plan is, for an organism, essentially the same as a program for a computer ... we regard a computer program that simulates certain features of an organism's behavior as a theory about the organismic Plan that generated the behavior.

Moreover, we shall also use the term "Plan" to designate a rough sketch of some course of action ... as well as the completely detailed specification of every detailed operation ... We shall say that a creature is executing a particular Plan when in fact that Plan is controlling the sequence of operations he is carrying out. (p. 17, original emphasis)

With Miller, Galanter, and Pribram, the view that purposeful action is planned is put forth as a psychological "process theory," compatible with the interest in a mechanistic, computationally tractable account of intelligent action. By improving upon or completing our common-sense descriptions of the structure of action, the structure is now represented not only as a plausible sequence, but as an hierarchical plan. The plan reduces, moreover, to a detailed set of instructions that actually serves as the program that controls the action. At this point, the plan as stipulated becomes substitutable for the action, insofar as the action is viewed as derivative from the plan. And once this substitution is done, the theory is self-sustaining: the problem of action is assumed to be solved by the planning model, and the task that remains is the model's refinement.

While attributing the plan to the actor resolves the question of the plan's status, however, it introduces new problems with respect to what we actually mean by "purposeful action." If plans are synonymous with purposeful action, how do we account, on the one hand, for a prior intent to act which may never be realized, and, on the other, for an intentional action for which we would ordinarily say no plan was formed ahead of time?[5] And if any plan of action can be analyzed at any level of detail, what level of description represents that which we would want to call purposeful action? If at every level, there is no reason in principle to distinguish, for example, between deliberate action and involuntary response, as the latter always can be ascribed to a process of planning unavailable to the actor. In fact, this is just what Boden would have us do. On her account, action can be reduced to basic units for which "no further procedural analysis could conceivably be given." Those units compose "complex procedural schemata or action-plans," which in turn produce "complex intentional effects" (1973, p. 36). Psychological processes at the level of intention, in other words, are reducible ultimately to bodily operations.

But while the planning model would have a statement of intent reflect an actual set of instructions for action, even casual observation indicates that our statements of intent generally do not address the question of situated action at any level of detail. In fact, because the relation of the intent to accomplish some goal to the actual course of situated action is enormously contingent, a statement of intent generally says very little about the action that follows. It is precisely because our plans are inherently vague – because we can state our intentions without having to describe the actual course that our actions will take – that an intentional vocabulary is so useful for our everyday affairs.

The confusion in the planning literature over the status of plans mirrors the fact that in our everyday action descriptions we do not normally distinguish between accounts of action provided before and after the fact, and action's actual course. As common-sense

[5] Davis (cited in Allen 1984) gives the example of a person driving who brakes when a small child runs in front of the car. See also Searle's distinction (1980) between "prior intentions" and "intentions-in-action."

constructs, plans are a constituent of practical action, but they are constituent as an artifact of our *reasoning about* action, not as the generative *mechanism of* action. Our imagined projections and our retrospective reconstructions are the principal means by which we catch hold of situated action and reason about it, while situated action itself, in contrast, is essentially transparent to us as actors.[6] The planning model, however, takes over our common-sense pre-occupation with the anticipation of action, and the review of its outcomes, and attempts to systematize that reasoning as a model for action itself, while ignoring the actual stuff, the situated action, which is the reasoning's object.

3.2 Speech acts

A growing number of research efforts devoted to machine intelligence have as their objective, for both theoretical and practical reasons, human–machine communication using English, or "natural language" (for example, Brady and Berwick 1983; Bruce 1981; Joshi, Webber, and Sag 1981). Researchers in natural language understanding have embraced Austin's observation (1962) that language is a form of action, as a way of subsuming communication to the planning model. If language is a form of action, it follows that language understanding, like the interpretation of action generally, involves an analysis of a speaker's utterances in terms of the plans those utterances serve:

> Let us start with an intuitive description of what we think occurs when one agent A asks a question of another agent B which B then answers. A has some *goal*; s/he creates a plan (*plan construction*) that involves asking B a question whose answer will provide some information needed in order to achieve the goal. A then executes this plan, asking B the

---

[6] One result of the transparency of situated action is that we have little vocabulary with which to talk about it, though chapters 4 and 5 attempt to present some recent efforts in social science. For a treatment of the philosophical vocabulary proposed by Heidegger, see Dreyfus, in press, ch. 6.

question. B interprets the question, and attempts to infer A's plan (*plan inference*). (Allen 1983, p. 110, original emphasis)

As with the interpretation of action, plans are the substrate on which the interpretation of natural language utterances rests, insofar as "[h]uman language behavior is part of a coherent plan of action directed toward satisfying a speaker's goals" (Appelt 1985, p. 1). We understand language, and action more generally, when we successfully infer the other's goals, and understand how the other's action furthers them. The appropriateness of a response turns on that analysis, from which, in turn:

> The hearer then adopts new goals (e.g., to respond to a request, to clarify the previous speaker's utterance or goal), and plans his own utterances to achieve those. A conversation ensues. (P. Cohen n.d., p. 24)

Given such an account of conversation, the research problem with respect to language understanding is essentially the same as that of the planning model more generally: that is, to characterize actions in terms of their preconditions and effects, and to formulate a set of inference rules for mapping between actions and underlying plans. Among researchers in the natural language area of artificial intelligence research, Searle's speech act theory (1969) is seen to offer some initial guidelines for computational models of communication:

> We hypothesize that people maintain, as part of their models of the world, symbolic descriptions of the world models of other people. Our plan-based approach will regard speech acts as operators whose effects are primarily on the models that speakers and hearers maintain of each other. (Cohen and Perrault 1979, p. 179)

Searle's conditions of satisfaction for the successful performance of speech acts are read as the speech act's "preconditions," while its illocutionary force is the desired "effect":

> Utterances are produced by actions (speech acts) that are ex-

ecuted in order to have some effect on the hearer. This effect typically involves modifying the hearer's beliefs or goals. A speech act, like any other action, may be observed by the hearer and may allow the hearer to infer what the speaker's plan is. (Allen 1983, p. 108)

In describing utterances by their preconditions and effects, speech acts seem to provide at least the framework within which computational mechanisms for engineering interaction between people and machines might emerge. But while Searle's "conditions of satisfaction" state conventions governing the illocutionary force of certain classes of utterance, he argues against the possibility of a rule-based semantics for construing the significance of any particular utterance. While the maxims that speech act theory proposes – for example, the felicity condition for a directive is that S wants H to do A – tell us something about the general conditions of satisfaction for a directive, they tell us nothing further about the significance of any particular directive. With respect to the problem of interpretation, Gumperz (1982b, p. 326) offers the following example from an exchange between two secretaries in a small office:

A: Are you going to be here for ten minutes?
B: Go ahead and take your break. Take longer if you want.
A: I'll just be outside on the porch. Call me if you need me.
B: OK. Don't worry.

Gumperz points out that B's response to A's question clearly indicates that B interprets the questions as an indirect request that B stay in the office while A takes a break, and, by her reply, A confirms that interpretation. B's interpretation accords with a categorization of A's question as an indirect speech act (Searle 1979), and with Grice's discussion of implicature (1975); i.e. B assumes that A is cooperating, and that her question must be relevant, therefore B searches her mind for some possible context or interpretive frame that would make sense of the question, and comes up with the break. But, Gumperz points out, *this analysis begs the question of how B arrives at the right inference*:

What is it about the situation that leads her to think A is talking about taking a break? A common sociolinguistic procedure in such cases is to attempt to formulate discourse rules such as the following: "If a secretary in an office around break time asks a co-worker a question seeking information about the co-worker's plans for the period usually allotted for breaks, interpret it as a request to take her break." Such rules are difficult to formulate and in any case are neither sufficiently general to cover a wide enough range of situations nor specific enough to predict responses. An alternative approach is to consider the pragmatics of questioning and to argue that questioning is semantically related to requesting, and that there are a number of contexts in which questions can be interpreted as requests. While such semantic processes clearly channel conversational inference, there is nothing in this type of explanation that refers to taking a break. (1982b, pp. 326–7)

The problem that Gumperz identifies here clearly applies equally to attempts to account for inferences such as B's by arguing that she "recognizes" A's plan to take a break. Clearly she does: the outstanding question is how. While we can always construct a *post hoc* account that explains interpretation in terms of knowledge of typical situations and motives, it remains the case that with speech act theory, as with the planning model, neither typifications of intent nor general rules for its expression are sufficient to account for the mutual intelligibility of our situated action. In the final analysis, attempts to construct a taxonomy of intentions and rules for their recognition seem to beg the question of situated interpretation, rather than answer it.

3.3 Background knowledge

Gumperz's example demonstrates a problem that any account of human action must face: namely, that an action's significance seems to lie as much in what it presupposes and implies about its situation, as in any explicit or observable behavior as such. Even the notion of observable behavior becomes problematic in this respect, insofar as what we do, and what we understand others to be doing, is so thoroughly informed by assumptions about the action's significance. In the interpretation of purposeful action, it is hard to know where the observation leaves off and where the interpretation begins. In recognition of the fact that human behavior is a figure defined by its ground, social science has largely turned from the observation of behavior to explication of the background that seems to lend behavior its sense.

For cognitive science, the background of action is not the world as such, but *knowledge* about the world. Researchers agree that representation of knowledge about the world is a principal limiting factor on progress in machine intelligence. The prevailing strategy in representing knowledge has been to categorize the world into domains of knowledge (e.g. areas of specialization, such as medicine, along one dimension, or propositions about physical phenomena, such as liquids, along another), and then to enumerate facts about the domain and relationships between them. Having carved out domains of specialized knowledge, the catch-all for anything not clearly assignable is "common sense," which then can be spoken of as if it were yet another domain of knowledge, albeit one that is foundational to the others.

While some progress has been made in selected areas of specialized knowledge, the domain of common-sense knowledge so far remains intractable and unwieldy. One approach to bounding common-sense knowledge, exemplified by the work of Schank and Abelson (1977), is to classify the everyday world as types of situations, and assign to each its own body of specialized knowledge. The claim is that our knowledge of the everyday world is organized by a "predetermined, stereotyped sequence of actions that define a well-known situation" or script (ibid., p. 422). Needless to say "[s]cripts are extremely numerous. There is a restaurant script, a birthday party script, a football game script, a classroom script, and so on" (p. 423). Every situation, in other words, has its plan made up of ordered action sequences, each action producing the conditions that enable the next action to occur. Admittedly, the normative order of these action sequences can be thrown off course, by any one of what Schank and Abelson term "distractions," "obstacles," or "errors." Distractions, about which they have little to say, comprise the interruption of one script by another, while:

> An obstacle to the normal sequence occurs when someone or something prevents a normal action from occurring or some enabling condition for the action is absent. An error occurs when the action is completed in an inappropriate manner, so that the normal consequences of the action do not come about. (p. 426)

Not only does the typical script proceed according to a normal sequence of actions, in other words, but each script has its typical obstacles and errors that, like the script itself, are stored in memory along with their remedies, and retrieved and applied as needed.

While plans associate intentions with action sequences, scripts associate action sequences with typical situations. In practice, however, the stipulation of relevant background knowledge for typical situations always takes the form of a partial list, albeit one offered as if the author could complete the list, given the requisite time and space:

> If one intends to buy bread, for instance, the knowledge of which bakers are open and which are shut on that day of the week will enter into the generation of one's plan of action in a definite way; one's knowledge of local topography (and perhaps of map-reading) will guide one's locomotion to the selected shop; one's knowledge of linguistic grammar and of the reciprocal roles of shopkeeper and customer will be needed to generate that part of the action-plan concerned

44

with speaking to the baker, and one's financial competence
will guide and monitor the exchange of coins over the shop
counter. (Boden 1973, p. 28)

Like Boden's story of the business of buying bread, attempts in artificial intelligence research to formalize common-sense knowledge
rely upon an appeal to intuition that shows little sign of yielding to
scientific methods. The difficulty is not just that every action presupposes a large quantity of background knowledge; though it
would pose practical problems, such a difficulty would be tractable
eventually. Just because "implicit knowledge" can in principle be
enumerated indefinitely, deciding in practice about the enumeration of background knowledge remains a stubbornly *ad hoc* procedure, for which researchers have not succeeded in constructing
rules that do not depend, in their turn, on some deeper *ad hoc* procedures.

Nevertheless, the image evoked by "shared knowledge" is a
potentially enumerable body of implicit assumptions or presuppositions that stands behind every explicit action or utterance, and
from which participants in interaction selectively draw in understanding each other's actions. This image suggests that what
actually does get said on any occasion must reflect the application
of a principle of communicative economy, which recommends
roughly that to the extent that either the premises or rationale of an
action can be assumed to be shared, they can be left unspoken. That
means, in turn, that speakers must have procedures for deciding
the extent of the listener's knowledge, and the commensurate requirements for explication. The listener, likewise, must make
inferences regarding the speaker's assumptions about shared
knowledge, on the basis of what he or she chooses explicitly to say.
What is unspoken and relevant to what is said is assumed to reside
in the speaker's and listener's common stock of background knowledge, the existence of which is proven by the fact that an account of
what is said always requires reference to further facts that, though
unspoken, are clearly relevant.

This image of communication is challenged, however, by the results of an exercise assigned by Garfinkel to his students (1972). Garfinkel's aim was to press the common-sense notion that background knowledge is a body of things thought but unsaid, that stands behind behavior and makes it intelligible. The request was that the students provide a complete description of what was communicated, in one particular conversation, as a matter of the participants' shared knowledge. Students were asked to report a simple conversation by writing on the left hand side of a piece of paper what was said, and on the right hand side what it was that they and their partners actually understood was being talked about. Garfinkel reports that when he made the assignment:

> many students asked how much I wanted them to write. As I progressively imposed accuracy, clarity, and distinctness, the task became increasingly laborious. Finally, when I required that they assume I would know what they had actually talked about only from reading literally what they wrote literally, they gave up with the complaint that the task was impossible. (p. 317)

The students' dilemma was not simply that they were being asked to write "everything" that was said, where that consisted of some bounded, albeit vast, content. It was rather that the task of enumerating what was talked about itself extended what was talked about, providing a continually receding horizon of understandings to be accounted for. The assignment, it turned out, was not to describe some existing content, but to generate it. As such, it was an endless task. The students' failure suggests not that they gave up too soon, but that what they were assigned to do was not what the participants in the conversation themselves did in order to achieve shared understanding.

While the notion of "background assumptions" connotes an actual collection of things that are there in the mind of the speaker – a body of knowledge that motivates a particular action or linguistic expression, and makes it interpretable – Garfinkel's exercise, as well as the phenomenology of experience, suggest that there is reason to question the view that background assumptions are part of the actor's mental state prior to action:

> As I dash out the door of my office, for example, I do not consciously entertain the belief that the floor continues on the other side, but if you stop me and ask me whether, when I charged confidently through the door, I believed that the floor continued on the other side, I would have to respond that indeed, I did. (Dreyfus 1982, p. 25)

A background assumption, in other words, is generated by the activity of accounting for an action when the premise of the action is called into question. But there is no particular reason to believe that the assumption actually characterizes the actor's mental state prior to the act. In this respect, the "taken for granted" denotes not a mental state but something outside of our heads that, precisely because it is non-problematically there, we do not need to think about. By the same token, in whatever ways we do find action to be problematical, the world is there to be consulted should we choose to do so. Similarly, we can assume the intelligibility of our actions, and as long as the others with whom we interact present no evidence of failing to understand us, we do not need to explain ourselves, yet the grounds and significance of our actions can be explicated endlessly. The situation of action is thus an inexhaustibly rich resource, and the enormous problems of specification that arise in cognitive science's theorizing about intelligible action have less to do with action than with the project of substituting definite procedures for vague plans, and representations of the situation of action, for action's actual circumstances.

To characterize purposeful action as in accord with plans and goals is just to say again that it is purposeful and that *somehow*, in a way not addressed by the characterization itself, we constrain and direct our actions according to the significance that we assign to a particular context. How we do that is the outstanding problem. Plans and goals do not provide the solution for that problem, they simply re-state it. The dependency of significance on a particular context, every particular context's open-endedness, and the essential *ad hoc*ness of contextual elaboration are resources for practical affairs, but perplexities for a science of human action. And, to anticipate the analysis in chapter 7, it is an intractable problem for projects that rest on providing in advance for the significance of canonical descriptions – such as instructions – for situated action.

4 Situated actions

> This total process [of Trukese navigation] goes forward
> without reference to any explicit principles and
> without any planning, unless the intention to proceed
> to a particular island can be considered a plan. It is non-
> verbal and does not follow a coherent set of logical
> steps. As such it does not represent what we tend to
> value in our culture as "intelligent" behavior.
>
> (Gladwin 1964, p. 175)

This chapter turns to recent efforts within anthropology and sociology to challenge traditional assumptions regarding purposeful
action and shared understanding. A point of departure for the challenge is the idea that common-sense notions of planning are not in-
adequate versions of scientific models of action, but rather are
resources for people's practical deliberations about action. As pro-
jective and retrospective accounts of action, plans are themselves
located in the larger context of some ongoing practical activity. As
common-sense notions about the structure of that activity, plans
are part of the subject matter to be investigated in a study of purposeful action, not something to be improved upon, or transformed
into axiomatic theories of action.

The premise that practical reasoning about action is properly part
of the subject matter of social studies is due to the emergence of a
branch of sociology named *ethnomethodology*. This chapter describes
the inversion of traditional social theory recommended by ethnomethodology, and the implications of that inversion for the problem of purposeful action and shared understanding. To designate
the alternative that ethnomethodology suggests – more a

49

reformulation of the problem of purposeful action, and a research programme, than an accomplished theory – I have introduced the term *situated action*. That term underscores the view that every course of action depends in essential ways upon its material and social circumstances. Rather than attempting to abstract action away from its circumstances and represent it as a rational plan, the approach is to study how people use their circumstances to achieve intelligent action. Rather than build a theory of action out of a theory of plans, the aim is to investigate how people produce and find evidence for plans in the course of situated action. More generally, rather than subsume the details of action under the study of plans, plans are subsumed by the larger problem of situated action.

The view of action that ethnomethodology recommends is neither behavioristic, in any narrow sense of that term, nor mentalistic. It is not behavioristic in that it assumes that the significance of action is not reducible to uninterpreted bodily movements. Nor is it mentalistic, however, in that the significance of action is taken to be based, in ways that are fundamental rather than secondary or epiphenomenal, in the physical and social world. The basic premise is twofold: first, that what traditional behavioral sciences take to be cognitive phenomena have an essential relationship to a publicly available, collaboratively organized world of artifacts and actions, and secondly, that the significance of artifacts and actions, and the methods by which their significance is conveyed, have an essential relationship to their particular, concrete circumstances.

The ethnomethodological view of purposeful action and shared understanding is outlined in this chapter under five propositions: (1) plans are representations of situated actions; (2) in the course of situated action, representation occurs when otherwise transparent activity becomes in some way problematic; (3) the objectivity of the situations of our action is achieved rather than given; (4) a central resource for achieving the objectivity of situations is language, which stands in a generally indexical relationship to the circumstances that it presupposes, produces, and describes; (5) as a consequence of the indexicality of language, mutual intelligibility is achieved on each occasion of interaction with reference to situation particulars, rather than being discharged once and for all by a stable body of shared meanings.

4.1 Plans are representations of action

The pragmatist philosopher and social psychologist George Herbert Mead (1934) has argued for a view of meaningful, directed action as two integrally but problematically related kinds of activity. One kind of activity is an essentially situated and *ad hoc* improvisation – the part of us, so to speak, that actually acts. The other kind of activity is derived from the first, and includes our representations of action in the form of future plans and retrospective accounts. Plans and accounts are distinguished from action as such by the fact that, to represent our actions, we must in some way make an object of them. Consequently, our descriptions of our actions come always before or after the fact, in the form of imagined projections and recollected reconstructions.

Mead's treatment of the relation of deliberation and reflection to action is one of the more controversial, and in some ways incoherent, pieces of his theory. But his premise of a disjunction between our actions and our grasp of them at least raises the question for social science of the relationship between projected or reconstructed courses of action, and actions *in situ*. Most accounts of purposeful action have taken this relationship to be a directly causal one, at least in a logical sense (see chapter 3). Given a desired outcome, the actor is assumed to make a choice among alternative courses of action, based upon the anticipated consequences of each with respect to that outcome. Accounts of actions taken, by the same token, are just a report on the choices made. The student of purposeful action on this view need know only the predisposition of the actor and the alternative courses that are available in order to predict the action's course. The action's course is just the playing out of these antecedent factors, knowable in advance of, and standing in a determinate relationship to, the action itself.

The alternative view is that plans are resources for situated action, but do not in any strong sense determine its course. While plans presuppose the embodied practices and changing circumstances of situated action, the efficiency of plans as representations comes precisely from the fact that they do not represent those practices and circumstances in all of their concrete detail. So, for example, in planning to run a series of rapids in a canoe, one is very likely to sit for a while above the falls and plan one's descent.[1] The plan might go something like "I'll get as far over to the left as possible, try to make it between those two large rocks, then backferry hard to the right to make it around that next bunch." A great deal of deliberation, discussion, simulation, and reconstruction may go into such a plan. But, however detailed, the plan stops short of the actual business of getting your canoe through the falls. When it really comes down to the details of responding to currents and handling a canoe, you effectively abandon the plan and fall back on whatever embodied skills are available to you. The purpose of the plan in this case is not to get your canoe through the rapids, but rather to orient you in such a way that you can obtain the best possible position from which to use those embodied skills on which, in the final analysis, your success depends.

Even in the case of more deliberative, less highly skilled activities, we generally do not anticipate alternative courses of action, or their consequences, until *some* course of action is already under way. It is frequently only on acting in a present situation that its possibilities become clear, and we often do not know ahead of time, or at least not with any specificity, what future state we desire to bring about. Garfinkel (1967) points out that in many cases it is only after we encounter some state of affairs that we find to be desirable that we identify that state as the goal toward which our previous actions, in retrospect, were directed "all along" or "after all" (p. 98). The fact that we can always perform a *post hoc* analysis of situated action that will make it appear to have followed a rational plan

---

[1] This example was suggested to me by Randy Trigg, to whom I am indebted for the insight that plans orient us for situated action in this way.

says more about the nature of our analyses than it does about our situated actions. To return to Mead's point, rather than direct situated action, rationality anticipates action before the fact, and reconstructs it afterwards.

4.2 *Representation and breakdown*

While we can always construct rational accounts of situated action before and after the fact, when action is proceeding smoothly it is essentially transparent to us. Similarly, when we use what Heidegger terms equipment that is "ready-to-hand," the equipment "has a tendency to 'disappear'":

> Consider the example (used by Wittgenstein and Merleau-Ponty) of the blind man's cane. We can hand the man the cane and ask him to tell us what properties it has. After hefting and feeling it, he can tell us that it is light, smooth, about three feet long, and so on; it is present-at-hand for him. But when the man starts to use the cane (when he grasps it in that special mode of understanding that Heidegger calls "manipulation") he loses his awareness of the cane itself; he is aware only of the curb (or whatever object the cane touches); or, if all is going well, he is not even aware of that. Thus it is that equipment that is ready-to-hand is invisible just when it is most genuinely appropriated. (Dreyfus, in press, ch. 6)

In contrast, the "unready-to-hand," in Heidegger's phrase, comprises occasions wherein equipment that is involved in some practical activity becomes unwieldy, temporarily broken, or unavailable. At such times, inspection and practical problem-solving occur, aimed at repairing or eliminating the disturbance in order to "get going again." In such times of disturbance, our use of equipment becomes "explicitly manifest as a goal-oriented activity," and we may then try to formulate procedures or rules:

> The scheme peculiar to [deliberating] is the "if-then"; if this

or that, for instance, is to be produced, put to use, or aver-
ted, then some ways and means, circumstances, or opportunities will be needed (Heidegger, cited in Dreyfus, in
press, ch. 6)

Another kind of breakdown, that arises when equipment to be
used is unfamiliar, is discussed in chapter 6 in relation to the
"expert help system" and the problem of instructing the novice
user of a machine. The important point here is just that the rules
and procedures that come into play when we deal with the
"unready-to-hand" are not self-contained or foundational, but contingent on and derived from the situated action that the rules and
procedures represent. The representations involved in managing
problems in the use of equipment presuppose the very transparent
practices that the problem renders noticeable or remarkable. Situated action, in other words, is not made explicit by rules and procedures. Rather, when situated action becomes in some way
problematic, rules and procedures are explicated for purposes of
deliberation and the action, which is otherwise neither rule-based
nor procedural, is then made accountable to them.

4.3 *The practical objectivity of situations*

If we look at the world commonsensically, the environment of our
actions is made up of a succession of situations that we walk in to,
and to which we respond. As I noted in chapter 3, advocates of the
planning model not only adopt this common-sense realist view
with respect to the individual actor, but attempt to bring concerted
action under the same account by treating the actions of others as
just so many more conditions of the actor's situation. In the same
tradition, normative sociology posits, and then attempts to describe, an objective world of social facts, or received norms, to
which our attitudes and actions are a response. Emile Durkheim's
famous maxim that "the objective reality of social facts is sociology's fundamental principle" (1938) has been the methodological

premise of social studies since early in this century. Recognizing the human environment to be constituted crucially by others, sociological norms comprise a set of environmental conditions beyond the material, to which human behavior is responsive: namely, the sanctions of institutionalized group life. Human action, the argument goes, cannot be adequately explained without reference to these "social facts," which are to be treated as antecedent, external, and coercive *vis-à-vis* the individual actor.

By adopting Durkheim's maxim, and assuming the individual's responsiveness to received social facts, social scientists hoped to gain respectability under the view that human responses to the facts of the social world should be discoverable by the same methods as are appropriate to studies of other organisms reacting to the natural world. A principal aim of normative sociology was to shift the focus of attention in studies of human behavior from the psychology of the individual to the conventions of the social group. But at the same time that normative sociology directed attention to the community or group, it maintained an image of the individual member rooted in behaviorist psychology and natural science – an image that has been dubbed by Garfinkel the "cultural dope":

> By "cultural dope" I refer to the man-in-the-sociologist's-society who produces the stable features of the society by acting in compliance with preestablished and legitimate alternatives of action that the common culture provides. (1967, p. 68)

Insofar as the alternatives of action that the culture provides are seen to be non-problematic and constraining on the individual, *their* enumeration is taken to constitute an account of situated human action. The social facts – that is to say, what actions typically come to – are used as a point of departure for retrospective theorizing about the "necessary character of the pathways whereby the end result is assembled" (p. 68).

In 1954, the sociologist Herbert Blumer published a critique of traditional sociology titled "What Is Wrong with Social Theory?" (see

Blumer 1969, pp. 140–52). Blumer argues that the social world is constituted by the local production of meaningful action, and that as such the social world has never been taken seriously by social scientists. Instead, Blumer says, investigations by social scientists have looked at meaningful action as the playing out of various determining factors, all antecedent and external to the action itself. Whether those factors are brought to the occasion in the form of individual predispositions, or are present in the situation as pre-existing environmental conditions or received social norms, the action itself is treated as epiphenomenal. As a consequence, Blumer argues, we have a social science that is about meaningful human action, but not a science of it.

For the foundations of a science of action, Blumer turns to Mead, who offers a metaphysics of action that is deeply sociological. Blumer points out that a central contribution of Mead's work is his challenge to traditional assumptions regarding the origins of the common-sense world, and of purposeful action:

> His treatment took the form of showing that human group life was the essential condition for the emergence of consciousness, the mind, a world of objects, human beings as organisms possessing selves, and human conduct in the form of constructed acts. He reversed the traditional assumptions underlying philosophical, psychological, and sociological thought to the effect that human beings possess minds and consciousness as original "givens," that they live in worlds of pre-existing and self-constituted objects, and that group life consists of the association of such reacting human organisms. (ibid., p. 61)

Mead's "reversal," in putting human interaction before the objectivity of the common-sense world, should not be read as an argument for metaphysical idealism; Mead does not deny the existence of constraints in the environment in which we act. What Mead is working toward is not a characterization of the natural world *simpliciter*, but of the natural world *under interpretation*, or the world as construed by us through language. The latter is precisely what we mean by the *social* world and, on Mead's account, interaction is a condition for that world, while that world is a condition for intentional action.

More recently, ethnomethodology has turned Durkheim's maxim on its head with more profound theoretical and methodological consequences. Briefly, the standpoint of ethnomethodology is that what traditional sociology captures is precisely our common-sense view of the social world (see Sacks 1963; Garfinkel 1967; and Garfinkel and Sacks 1970). Following Durkheim, the argument goes, social studies have simply taken this common-sense view as foundational, and attempted to build a science of the social world by improving upon it. Social scientific theories, under this attempt, are considered to be scientific insofar as they remedy shortcomings in, and preferably quantify, the intuitions of everyday, practical sociological reasoning.

In contrast, ethnomethodology grants common-sense sociological reasoning a fundamentally different status than that of a defective approximation of an adequate scientific theory. Rather than being *resources* for social science to improve upon, the "all things being equal" typifications of common-sense reasoning are to be taken as social science's *topic*. The notion that we act in response to an objectively given social world is replaced by the assumption that our everyday social practices render the world publicly available and mutually intelligible. It is those practices that constitute ethnomethods. The methodology of interest to ethnomethodologists, in other words, is not their own, but that deployed by members of the society in coming to know, and making sense out of, the everyday world of talk and action.

The outstanding question for social science, therefore, is not whether social facts are objectively grounded, but how that objective grounding is accomplished. Objectivity is a product of systematic practices, or members' methods for rendering our unique experience and relative circumstances mutually intelligible. The source of mutual intelligibility is not a received conceptual scheme, or a set of coercive rules or norms, but those common practices that produce the typifications of which schemes and rules are made. The task of social studies, then, is to describe the practices, not to enumerate their product in the form of a catalogue of common-sense beliefs about the social world. The interest of ethnomethodologists, in other words, is in how it is that the mutual intelligibility and objectivity of the social world is achieved. Ethnomethodology locates that achievement in our everyday situated actions, such that our common sense of the social world is not the precondition for our interaction, but its product. By the same token, the objective reality of social facts is not the fundamental *principle* of social studies, but social studies' fundamental *phenomenon*.

4.4 The indexicality of language

Our shared understanding of situations is due in great measure to the efficiency of language, "the typifying medium *par excellence*" (Schultz 1962, p. 14). The efficiency of language is due to the fact that, on the one hand, expressions have assigned to them conventional meanings, which hold on any occasion of their use. The significance of a linguistic expression on some actual occasion, on the other hand, lies in its relationship to circumstances that are presupposed or indicated by, but not actually captured in, the expression itself.[2] Language takes its significance from the embedding world, in other words, even while it transforms the world into something that can be thought of and talked about.

Expressions that rely upon their situation for significance are commonly called *indexical*, after the "indexes" of Charles Peirce (1933), the exemplary indexicals being first- and second-person pronouns, tense, and specific time and place adverbs such as "here" and "now." In the strict sense exemplified by these commonly recognized indexical expressions, the distinction of conventional or literal meaning, and situated significance, breaks down. That is to say, these expressions are distinguished by the fact that

[2] For a semantic theory based on this view of language, see Barwise and Perry 1985.

while one can state procedures for finding the expression's significance, or rules for its use, the expression's meaning can be specified only as the use of those procedures in some actual circumstances (see Bates 1976, ch. 1).

Heritage (1984) offers as an example the indexical expression "that's a nice one" (p. 143). There is, first of all, the obvious fact that this expression will have quite a different significance when uttered by a visitor with reference to a photograph in her host's photo album, or by one shopper to another in front of the lettuce bin at the grocery store. But while linguists and logicians would commonly recognize the referent of "that's" as the problematic element in such cases, Heritage points out that the significance of the descriptor "nice" is equally so. So, in the first case, "nice" will refer to some properties of the photograph, while different properties will be intended in the case of the lettuce. Moreover, in either case whichever sense of "nice" is intended is not available from the utterance, but remains to be found by the hearer through an active search of both the details of the referent, and the larger context of the remark. So "nice" in the first instance might be a comment on the composition of the photograph, or on the appearance of the host, or on some indefinite range of other properties of the photo in question. What is more, visitor and host will never establish in just so many words precisely what it is that the visitor intends and the host understands. Their interpretations of the term will remain partially unarticulated, located in their unique relationship to the photograph and the context of the remark. Yet the shared understanding that they do achieve will be perfectly adequate for purposes of their interaction. It is in this sense – that is, that expression and interpretation involve an active process of pointing to and searching the situation of talk – that language is a form of situated action.

Among philosophers and linguists, the term "indexicality" typically is used to distinguish those classes of expressions whose meaning is conditional on the situation of their use in this way from those such as, for example, definite noun phrases whose meaning is claimed to be specifiable in objective, or context-independent terms. But the *communicative* significance of a linguistic expression is always dependent upon the circumstances of its use. A formal statement not of what the language means in relation to any context, but of what the language-user means in relation to some particular context, requires a description of the context or situation of the utterance itself. And every utterance's situation comprises an indefinite range of possibly relevant features. Our practical solution to this theoretical problem is not to enumerate some subset of the relevant circumstances – we generally never mention our circumstances as such at all – but to "wave our hand" at the situation, as if we always included in our utterance an implicit *ceteris paribus* clause, and closed with an implicit et cetera clause. One consequence of this practice is that we always "mean more than we can say in just so many words":

> [S]peakers can ... do the immense work that they do with natural language, even though over the course of their talk it is not known and is never, not even "in the end," available for saying in so many words just what they are talking about. Emphatically, that does not mean that speakers do not know what they are talking about, *but instead that they know what they are talking about in that way*. (Garfinkel and Sacks 1970, pp. 342–4, original emphasis)

In this sense deictic expressions, time and place adverbs, and pronouns are just particularly clear illustrations of the general fact that all situated language, including the most abstract or eternal, stands in an essentially indexical relationship to the embedding world.

Because the significance of an expression always exceeds the meaning of what actually gets said, the interpretation of an expression turns not only on its conventional or definitional meaning, nor on that plus some body of presuppositions, but on the unspoken situation of its use. Our situated use of language, and consequently language's significance, presupposes and implies an horizon of things that are never actually mentioned – what Schutz referred to as the "world taken for granted" (1962, p. 74). Philosophers have been preoccupied with this fact about language as a matter of the truth conditionality of propositions, the problem being that the truth conditions of an assertion are always relative to a background, and the background does not form part of the semantic content of the sentence as such (Searle 1979). And the same problems that have plagued philosophers of language as a matter of principle are now practical problems for cognitive science. As I pointed out in chapter 3, the view that mutual intelligibility rests on a stock of shared knowledge has been taken over by researchers in cognitive science, in the hope that an enumeration of the knowledge assumed by particular words or actions could be implemented as data structures in the machine, which would then "understand" those words and actions. Actual attempts to include the background assumptions of a statement as part of its semantic content, however, run up against the fact that there is no fixed set of assumptions that underlies a given statement. As a consequence, the elaboration of background assumptions is fundamentally *ad hoc* and arbitrary, and each elaboration of assumptions in principle introduces further assumptions to be elaborated, *ad infinitum*.

The problem of communicating instructions for action, in particular certain of its seemingly intractable difficulties, becomes clearer with this view of language in mind. The relation of efficient linguistic formulations to particular situations parallels the relation of instructions to situated action. As linguistic expressions, instructions are subject to the constraint that:

> However extensive or explicit what a speaker says may be, it does not by its extensiveness or explicitness pose a task of deciding the correspondence between what he says and what he means that is resolved by citing his talk verbatim. (Garfinkel and Sacks 1970, pp. 342–4)

This indexicality of instructions means that an instruction's significance with respect to action does not inhere in the instruction, but must be found by the instruction follower with reference to the situation of its use. Far from replacing the *ad hoc* methods used to establish the significance of everyday talk and action, therefore, the interpretation of instructions is thoroughly reliant on those same methods:

> To treat instructions as though *ad hoc* features in their use was a nuisance, or to treat their presence as grounds for complaining about the incompleteness of instructions, is very much like complaining that if the walls of a building were gotten out of the way, one could see better what was keeping the roof up. (Garfinkel 1967, p. 22)

Like all action descriptions, instructions necessarily rely upon an implicit et cetera clause in order to be called complete. The project of instruction-writing is ill conceived, therefore, if its goal is the production of exhaustive action descriptions that can guarantee a particular interpretation. What "keeps the roof up" in the case of instructions for action is not only the instructions as such, but their interpretation in use. And the latter has all of the *ad hoc* and uncertain properties that characterize every occasion of the situated use of language.

4.5 *The mutual intelligibility of action*

By "index," Peirce meant not only that the sign relies for its significance on the event or object that it indicates, but also that the sign is actually a constituent of the referent. So situated language more generally is not only anchored in, but in large measure constitutes, the situation of its use. Ethnomethodology generalizes this constitutive function of language still further to action, in the proposition that the purposefulness of action is recognizable in virtue of the methodic, skillful, and therefore taken-for-granted practices whereby we establish the rational properties of actions in a particular context. It is those practices that provide for the "analyzability of actions-in-context given that not only does no concept of context-in-general exist, but every use of 'context' without exception is itself essentially indexical" (Garfinkel 1967, p. 10).

In positing the reflexivity of purposeful action and the methods by which we convey and construe action's purposes, ethnomethodology does not intend to reduce meaningful action to method. The intent is rather to identify the mutual intelligibility of action as *the* problem for sociology. To account for the foundations of mutual intelligibility and social order, traditional social science posits a system of known-in-common social conventions or behavioral norms. What we share, on this view, is agreement on the appropriate relation of actions to situations. We walk into a situation, identify its features, and match our actions to it. This implies that, on any given occasion, the concrete situation must be recognizable as an instance of a class of typical situations, and the behavior of the actor must be recognizable as an instance of a class of appropriate actions. And with respect to communication, as Wilson (1970) points out:

> the different participants must define situations and actions in essentially the same way, since otherwise rules could not operate to produce coherent interaction over time. Within the normative paradigm, this cognitive agreement is provided by the assumption that the actors share a system of culturally established symbols and meanings. Disparate definitions of situations and actions do occur, of course, but these are handled as conflicting subcultural traditions or idiosyncratic deviations from the culturally established cognitive consensus. (p. 699)

In contrast with this normative paradigm, Garfinkel proposes that the stability of the social world is not the consequence of a "cognitive consensus," or stable body of shared meanings, but of our tacit use of the documentary method of interpretation to find the coherence of situations and actions. As a general process, the documentary method describes a search for uniformities that underlie unique appearances. Applied to the social world, it describes the process whereby actions are taken as evidence, or "documents," of underlying plans or intent, which in turn fill in the sense of the actions (1967, ch. 3). The documentary method describes an ability – the ascription of intent on the basis of evidence, and the interpretation of evidence on the basis of ascribed intent – that is as identifying of rationality as the ability to act rationally itself. At the same time, the documentary method is not reducible to the application of any necessary and sufficient conditions, either behavioral or contextual, for the identification of intent. There are no logical formulae for recognizing the intent of some behavior independent of context, and there are no recognition algorithms for joining contextual particulars to behavioral descriptions so that forms of intent can be precisely defined over a set of necessary and sufficient observational data (see Coulter 1983, pp. 162–3).

Given the lack of universal rules for the interpretation of action, the programme of ethnomethodology is to investigate and describe the use of the documentary method in particular situations. Studies indicate, on the one hand, the generality of the method and, on the other, the extent to which special constraints on its use characterize specialized domains of practical activity, such as natural science, courts of law, and the practice of medicine.[3] In a contrived situation that, though designed independently and not with them in mind, closely parallels both the "Turing test" and encounters with Weizenbaum's ELIZA programs, Garfinkel set out to test the documentary method in the context of counseling. Students were asked to direct questions concerning their personal problems to someone they knew to be a student counselor, seated in another room. They were restricted to questions that could take yes/no answers, and the answers were then given by the counselor on a random basis. For the students, the counselor's answers were motivated by the questions. That is to say, by taking each answer as evidence for

[3] For example, the work of coroners at the Los Angeles Suicide Prevention Center (Garfinkel 1967, pp. 11–18), the deliberations of juries (ibid., ch. 4) and courtroom practices of attorneys (Atkinson and Drew 1979), the work of clinic staff in selecting patients for out-patient psychiatric treatment (Garfinkel 1967, ch. 7), the work of physicians interviewing patients for purposes of diagnosis (Beckman and Frankel 1983), the work of scientists discovering an optical pulsar (Garfinkel, Lynch, and Livingston 1981).

what the counselor "had in mind," the students were able to find a deliberate pattern in the exchange that explicated the significance and relevance of each new response as an answer to their question. Specifically, the yes/no utterances were found to document advice from the counselor, intended to help in the solution of the student's problem. So, for example, students assigned to the counselor, as the advice "behind" the answer, the thought formulated in the student's question:

> when a subject asked "Should I come to school every night after supper to do my studying?" and the experimenter said "My answer is no," the subject in his comments said, "He said I shouldn't come to school and study." (Garfinkel 1967, p. 92).

In cases where an answer seemed directly to contradict what had come before, students either attributed the apparent contradiction to a change of mind on the part of the counselor, as the result of having learned more between the two replies, or to some agenda on the part of the counselor that lent the reply a deeper significance than its first, apparently inconsistent, interpretation would suggest. In other cases, the interpretation of previous answers was revised in light of the current one, or an interpretation of the question was found, and attributed to the counselor, that rationalized what would otherwise appear to be an inappropriate answer. Generally:

> The underlying pattern was elaborated and compounded over the series of exchanges and was accommodated to each present "answer" so as to maintain the "course of advice," to elaborate what had "really been advised" previously, and to motivate the new possibilities as emerging features of the problem. (p. 90)

Garfinkel's results with arbitrary responses make the success of Weizenbaum's DOCTOR program easier to understand, and lend support to Weizenbaum's hypothesis that the intelligence of interactions with the DOCTOR program is due to the work of the human participant – specifically, to methods for interpreting the system's behavior as evidence for some underlying intent. The larger implications of the documentary method, however, touch on the status of an "underlying" reality of psychological and social facts in human interaction, prior to situated action and interpretation:

> It is not unusual for professional sociologists to think of their ... procedures as processes of "seeing through" appearances to an underlying reality; of brushing past actual appearances to "grasp the invariant." Where our subjects are concerned, their processes are not appropriately imagined as "seeing through," but consist instead of coming to terms with a situation in which factual knowledge of social structures – factual in the sense of warranted grounds of further inferences and actions – must be assembled and made available for potential use despite the fact that the situations it purports to describe are, in any calculable sense, unknown; in their actual and intended logical structures are essentially vague; and are modified, elaborated, extended, if not indeed created, by the fact and matter of being addressed. (Garfinkel 1967, p. 96)

The stability of the social world, from this standpoint, is not due to an eternal structure, but to situated actions that create and sustain shared understanding on specific occasions of interaction. Social constraints on appropriate action are always identified relative to some unique and unreproducible set of circumstances. Members of the society are treated as being at least potentially aware of the concrete detail of their circumstances, and their actions are interpreted in that light. Rather than actions being *determined by* rules, actors effectively *use* the normative rules of conduct that are available to produce significant actions. So, for example, there is a normative rule for greetings which runs to the effect: do not initiate greetings except with persons who are acquaintances. If we witness a person greeting another who we know is not an acquaintance, we can either conclude that the greeter broke the rule, or we can infer that, via the use of the rule, he or she was seeking to treat the other as an acquaintance (Heritage 1984, p. 126). Such rules are not taught or encoded, but are learned tacitly through typification over families of similar situations and actions.

Despite the availability of such typifications, no action can fully provide for its own interpretation in any given instance. Instead, every instance of meaningful action must be accounted for separately, with respect to specific, local, contingent determinants of significance. The recommendation for social studies, as a consequence, is that instead of looking for a structure that is invariant across situations, we look for the processes whereby particular, uniquely constituted circumstances are systematically interpreted so as to render meaning shared and action accountably rational. Structure, on this view, is an emergent product of situated action, rather than its foundation. Insofar as the project of ethnomethodology is to redirect social science from its traditional preoccupation with abstract structures to an interest in situated actions, and the cognitive sciences share in that same tradition, the ethnomethodological project has implications for cognitive science as well.

5 *Communicative resources*

Thus the whole framework of conversational constraints ... can become something to honor, to invert,
or to disregard, depending as the mood strikes.

(Goffman 1975, p. 311)

Communicative action occurs in particular moments of
actual time, in particular relationships of simultaneity
and sequence. These relationships in time, taken
together, constitute a regular rhythmic pattern. This
regularity in time and timing seems to play an essential, constitutive role in the social organization of interaction... Whereas there is no metronome playing
while people talk, their talking itself serves as a metronome.   (Erickson and Shultz 1982, p. 72)

We are environments for each other.

(McDermott 1976, p. 27)

An argument of the preceding chapter was that we never definit-
ively determine the intent behind an action, in that descriptions at
the level of intent are not designed to pick out mental states that
stand in some relation of strict causality to action, or even, in any
strong sense, of one-to-one correspondence. Instead, intentional
descriptions classify over situations and actions, as typifications
that invariably include an "open horizon of unexplored content"
(Schutz 1962, p. 14). In spite of this inherent indeterminacy, intentional descriptions not only suffice to classify purposeful behavior
but, given the unique and fleeting circumstances of situated action,
and the need to represent it efficiently, seem ideally suited to the
task. Attributing intent in any particular instance, moreover, is

68

generally non-problematic, even transparent, for members of the society who, from their practical perspective and for their practical purposes, are engaged in the everyday business of making sense out of each others' actions. When disputes over the significance of an action do arise, the uncertainty of intentional attributions becomes a practical problem, but in such cases it is the "right" interpretation of the action, not the fact of its inherent uncertainty, that is of interest to participants.

For students of purposeful action, however, the observation that action interpretation is inherently uncertain does have a methodological consequence: namely, it recommends that we turn our focus from explaining away uncertainty in the interpretation of action to identifying the resources by which the inevitable uncertainty is managed. A central tenet of social studies of practical action is that those resources are not only cognitive, but interactional. While acknowledging the role of conventional meanings and individual predispositions in mutual intelligibility, therefore, this chapter focuses on the neglected other side of shared understanding: namely the local, interactional work that produces intelligibility, *in situ*. The starting premise is that interpreting the significance of action is an essentially collaborative achievement. Rather than depend upon reliable recognition of intent, mutual intelligibility turns on the availability of communicative resources to detect, remedy, and at times even exploit the inevitable uncertainties of action's significance.

In order to underscore the breadth and subtlety of the resources available for shared understanding, and the precision of their use, this chapter focuses on the richest form of human communication, face-to-face interaction. The premise of conversation analyses (see Heritage 1985 for a comprehensive review) is that face-to-face interaction incorporates the broadest range of possible resources for communication, with other forms of interaction being characterizable in terms of particular resource limitations or additional constraints (see Sacks, Schegloff, and Jefferson 1978). In the discussion that follows I consider only a small subset of these resources; for example, I do not include the wealth of prosodic and gestural cues described by students of interaction. The rationale for neglecting those cues here, and in the analysis of chapter 7, is that the case of human–machine interaction is so limited that the basic resources, let alone the expressive subtleties, of human interaction are in question. Sections 5.1–5.3 describe the resources of the most unrestricted form of face-to-face interaction, everyday conversation. In section 5.4, I consider some modifications to everyday conversation that have developed for specialized purposes in institutional settings and, in chapter 6, some additional constraints introduced by restrictions on the mutual access of participants to each other and to a common situation. Finally, human–machine communication is analyzed, in chapter 7, as an extreme form of resource-limited interaction.

5.1 Conversation as "ensemble" work

The most common view of conversation is that speakers and listeners, pursuing some common topic according to individual predispositions and agendas, engage in an alternating sequence of action and response. For students of human cognition and of language, conversation generally has been treated as epiphenomenal with respect to the central concerns of their fields. Cognitively, conversation is just the meeting ground of individual psychologies, while linguistically it is the noisy, real-world occasion for the exercise of basic language abilities. On either view, the additional constraints imposed by situated language are a complication that obscures the underlying structure of cognitive or linguistic competence. As a consequence, linguists generally have not used actual speech for the analysis of linguistic competence, on the assumption that the phrasal breaks, restarts, hesitations, and the like found in actual speech represent such a defective performance that the data are of no use. And in analyzing idealized utterances, linguists have focused exclusively on the speaker's side in the communicative process (Streeck 1980). When one takes situated language as the subject matter, however, the definition of the field must necessarily shift to communication under naturally occurring circumstances. And when one moves back far enough from the utterances of the speaker to bring the listener into view as well, it appears that much in the actual construction of situated language that has been taken to reflect problems of speaker performance, instead reflects speaker competence in responding to cues provided by the listener (C. Goodwin 1981, pp. 12–13).

Closer analyses of face-to-face communication indicate that conversation is not so much an alternating series of actions and reactions between individuals as it is a joint action accomplished through the participants' continuous engagement in speaking and listening (see Schegloff 1972, 1982; C. Goodwin 1981). In contrast to the prevailing preoccupation of linguists and discourse analysts with speaking, where the listener is largely taken for granted or as extraneous, conversation analysis shows that the action of listening is consequential to the extent that

> the listener's failure to act at the right time in the right way literally prevents the speaker from finishing what he was trying to say – at least from finishing it in the way he was previously saying it. The speaker, in continuing to speak socially (i.e. in taking account in speaking of what the other is doing in listening), makes *accountable* the listener's violations of expectations for appropriate listening behavior. (Erickson and Shultz 1982, pp. 118–19, original emphasis)

In the same way that the listener attends to the speaker's words and actions in order to understand them, in other words, the speaker takes the behavior of the listener as evidence for the listener's response. Schegloff (1982, p. 72) offers the example of the lecturer:

> Anyone who has lectured to a class knows that the (often silent) reactions of the audience – the wrinkling of brows at some point in its course, a few smiles or chuckles or nods, or their absence – can have marked consequences for the talk

71

which follows: whether, for example, the just preceding point is reviewed, elaborated, put more simply, etc., or whether the talk moves quickly on to the next point, and perhaps to a more subtle point than was previously planned.

The local resources or *contextualization cues* by which people produce the mutual intelligibility of their interaction consist in the systematic organization of speech prosody (Gumperz 1982a), body position and gesture (Birdwhistell 1970; Erickson 1982; Scheflen 1974, gaze (C. Goodwin 1981; M. Goodwin 1980), and the precision of collaboratively accomplished timing (Erickson and Shultz 1982). For example, Erickson and Shultz suggest that what may be disturbing about certain speaker hesitations in conversation is not so much the interruption of talk as such, but the fact that, when talk stops and starts in temporally unpredictable ways, it is difficult for listeners to coordinate their listening actions (1982, p. 114). The richness of both simultaneous and sequential coordination

> suggests that conversational inference is best seen not as a simple unitary evaluation of intent but as involving a complex series of judgments, including relational or contextual assessments on how items of information are to be integrated into what we know and into the event at hand. (Gumperz 1982b, pp. 328–9)

As with any skill, in ordinary conversation these judgments are made with such proficiency that they are largely transparent, though at times of breakdown they may become contestable (see Gumperz and Tannen 1979). Viewed as highly skilled performance, the organization of conversation appears to be closer to what in playing music is called "ensemble" work (Erickson and Shultz 1982, p. 71) than it is to the common notion of speaker stimulus and listener response.

5.2 *Conversational organization*

One reason to begin a consideration of interaction with the organization of conversation is that studies of everyday conversation, and more recently studies in specific institutional settings where the type, distribution, and content of turns at talk are constrained in characteristic ways (see 5.4), indicate that all of the various forms of talk (e.g. interviews, cross-examinations, lectures, formal debates, and so on) can be viewed as modifications to conversation's basic structure (see Sacks, Schegloff, and Jefferson 1978). As the basic system for situated communication, conversation is characterized by (1) an organization designed to support local, "endogenous" control over the development of topics or activities, and to maximize accommodation of unforseeable circumstances that arise, and (2) resources for locating and remedying the communication's troubles as part of its fundamental organization.

5.2.1 Local control

Taking ordinary conversation as their subject matter Sacks, Schegloff, and Jefferson (1978) set out to identify the structural mechanisms by which this most "unstructured" of human activities is accomplished in a systematic and orderly way. Two problems for any interaction are the distribution of access to "the floor" and, closely related, control over the development of the topic or activity at hand. In contrast to mechanisms that administer an *a priori*, externally imposed agenda (for example, the format for a debate), the organization of conversation maximizes local control over both the distribution of turns and the direction of subject matter. That is to say, who talks and what gets talked about is decided then and there, by the participants in the conversation, through their collaborative construction of the conversation's course.

That turn-taking is a collaborative achievement, rather than a simple alternation of intrinsically bounded segments of talk, is evident in the common occurrence in actual conversation of simultaneous talk, of joint production of a single sentence, and of silence. The observations that somehow one speaker only takes the floor when two begin together, that a listener may finish the speaker's turn without it constituting an interruption, and that any participant in a conversation, including the last to speak, may begin a new turn out of silence, raise theoretical questions about the proper definition of a turn's boundaries and the process by which turn transitions are organized (see C. Goodwin 1981, p. 2). In answer to such questions, Sacks, Schegloff, and Jefferson (1978) have delineated a set of conventions or normative rules by which turn-taking is accomplished. By "normative" is meant only that these rules describe common practices observed by analysts of conversation. Speakers and listeners do not "know" these rules in the sense that they would or could formulate them in so many words. Rather, it can be seen by an observer, having these rules in mind, that they describe the practices by which people in conversation achieve the orderly distribution of turns.

The set of rules for turn-taking provides that for every place in the course of an utterance that is a projectable completion point for the utterance, one of the following occurs:

(a) the current speaker selects a next speaker, e.g., by directing a question or other implicative utterance at a particular hearer;
(b) another participant self-selects, by being the first to start speaking;
(c) the current speaker continues.

Options (a)–(c) are not simply alternatives, but an ordered set. That is to say, at each place where a transition to a new speaker might be effected, the rule set applies as a matter of "if not (a), then (b) is an option," "if not (b), then (c) is an option" recursively until a change in speaker occurs. This does not mean, of course, that participants wait to see which rule applies and then act accordingly – the options are theirs to exercise, they are not the workings of some external mechanism. Moreover, the rules are not necessarily, but contingently, applied. Which rule will prevail in any given case is determined by actions taken by the participants at each possible

74

turn-transition place, and the contingency of the rules means that the exercise of each is constrained by the presence of the others in the set independently of their actually being employed on any given occasion. Lower priority options constrain higher priority options – for example, for the (b) option to be exercised given the presence of (c), it will need to be employed before (c) is invoked, at which time priority returns to (a).

Due to the ordering of the rule set, the system for turn-taking constrains both the way that current speakers develop their talk and the way that others listen. Most obviously, the current speaker has reason to let listeners know where he or she is in the turn's course. This may be done explicitly, through introductions on the order of "I want to say a couple of things," or through the use of story prefaces which announce the onset of an extended multi-sentence turn with its own distinctive shape (see Sacks 1974). More implicitly, the speaker's control of the floor offers some inherent advantage. In order to preclude the exercise of option (b) before having had a say, the current speaker can extend his or her turn by, for example, withholding a point until after supporting arguments have been made.

The speaker does not define the turn unilaterally, however: turn completion is as much a function of the listener's inclination to respond as it is a matter of the speaker's readiness to yield. The units of which turns are constructed are expandable, not fixed – any unit from a particle to an extended exposition may constitute a turn – and what happens at each possible turn-transition place is contingent on the actions of participants other than the speaker. So, for example, by passing on option (b) at a possible transition place listeners may invite the speaker to continue, turning what could be a speaker change into a pause in the same speaker's turn. Or listeners may, on finding in either the speaker's exercise of option (a), or failure to exercise option (c), that a turn is completed, then look back over what was said in order to respond to it.

Because each projectable point of completion is a possible place for speaker change, the turn is essentially interactionally

determined over the course of the conversation. And rather than relying on a discrete set of "turn-yielding signals" (Duncan 1974),
speaker continuity or change is managed with reference to the
same range of syntactic, semantic, and non-linguistic resources by
which participants construct the significance of what is being said:

> By virtue of its character, it is misconceived to treat turns as
> units characterized by a division of labor in which the
> speaker determines the unit and its boundaries, and other
> parties to the conversation have as their task the recognition
> of them. Rather, the turn is a unit whose constitution and
> boundaries involve such a distribution of tasks (as we have
> noted): That a speaker can talk in such a way as to permit
> projection of possible completion to be made from his talk,
> and to allow others to use its transition places to start talk, to
> pass up talk, to affect directions of talk, and so on, and that
> their starting to talk, if properly placed, can determine
> where he ought to stop talk. (Sacks, Schegloff, and Jefferson
> 1978, p. 42)

The interactional structure of turn-taking presents some distinctive problems for the definition and categorization of units in conversational analysis. For example, one might argue reasonably that
silence should be classified differently according to whether it
occurs within the turn of a single speaker (a pause), or between
turns of different speakers (a gap) (C. Goodwin 1981, p. 18). The
problem that arises for analysts is exemplified, however, in a case
such as the following:[1]

John: Well I, I took this course.
        (0.5)
Ann: In how to quit?
            [
John: which I really recommend.

---

[1] C. Goodwin 1981, p. 18. Transcripts are presented here with the notation and
punctuation of the original source. A full description of the notation system (based
on Jefferson 1984) can be found at the end of the chapter.

The ambiguous status of the silence in this example as either a pause or a gap is not so much an analytic problem as it is an inherent property of situated talk. That is to say, the silence is treated by Ann as a gap, by John as a pause, such that "the same silence yields alternative classifications at different moments in time from the perspective of different participants" (p. 19). No single classification of the silence will do, as its status is inextricably tied to an event developing over time, and is subject to transformation. From Ann's point of view, at the point where she begins to speak, John's turn appears to be complete. John's extension of the turn, however, makes the silence into a pause, and Ann's turn into an interruption that begins in the midst, rather than at the completion of, his utterance. The status of what constitutes John's "turn" in this exchange, and therefore the status of the silence, is essentially ambiguous in a way that will not be remedied by any exercise of the analyst. To the contrary, attempts to remedy the ambiguity must do damage to the phenomenon which is precisely that boundaries of a turn are mutable, and that the structure of conversation is achieved by speakers and hearers in this locally developing, contingent way.

As a consequence of its interactional nature, the turn is not the kind of object that can be first defined and then examined for how it is passed back and forth between speakers. Instead, intrinsic structural elements of the turn are contingent on the process by which control changes hands between participants in conversation, as is the structure of the conversation produced. The point is not just that speakers can extend the length of their turns by the addition of further units of speech, but that through that essentially transparent mechanism they are able to change the emerging meaning of their talk within a turn to fit the actions of their listener (see C. Goodwin 1981, p. 11). The localness of the constraints on speakers' constructions of turns-at-talk, and the turn's contingency on the actions of other speakers, make conversation maximally sensitive and adaptable to particular participants and to unforeseen circumstances of the developing interaction. The turn-taking system for

77

conversation demonstrates how a system for communication that accommodates any participants, under any circumstances, may be systematic and orderly, while it must be essentially *ad hoc*.

5.2.2 *Sequential organization and coherence*

In addition to providing a mechanism for control over the distribution of turns, the turn-taking system bears a direct relation to the control of inferences about the conversation's content. In general, a coherent conversation is one in which each thing said can be heard as relevant to what has come before. Most locally, this means that the relevance of a turn is conditional on that which immediately precedes it:

> By conditional relevance of one item on another we mean; given the first, the second is expectable; upon its occurrence it can be seen to be a second item to the first; upon its non-occurrence it can be seen to be officially absent. (Schegloff 1972, p. 364)

Two utterances that stand in a relationship of conditional relevance of one on the other, in this local sense, constitute an *adjacency pair* in Schegloff and Sacks's terminology (1973), though conditional relevance is not limited to literal adjacency (see Levinson 1983, p. 304). The first part of an adjacency pair both sets up an expectation with respect to what should come next, and directs the way in which what does come next is heard (Schegloff 1972, p. 367). By the same token, the absence of an expected second part is a notable absence, and therefore takes on significance as well. In this way silences, for example, can be meaningful – most obviously, a silence following an utterance that implicates a response will be "heard" as belonging to the recipient of the utterance, and as a failure to respond. Similarly, a turn that holds the place of the second part of an adjacency pair, but cannot be made relevant to the first, will be seen as a *non sequitur*, or as incoherent.

The conditional relevance of adjacency pairs is an instance of what we might call, following Durkheim, a "social fact." The first part of an adjacency pair constrains the second part in a double sense. The constraint is not only a matter of the coherence or intelligibility of the second part, but also of the accountability of the respondent for inferences that the *absence* of a second part would warrant. For example, in the case of interactions opened by a summons, such as calling someone's name or ringing her doorbell:

> A member of the society may not "naively choose" not to answer a summons. The culture provides that a variety of "strong inferences" can be drawn from the fact of the official absence of an answer, and any member who does not answer does so at the peril of one of those inferences being made ... although members can, indeed "choose" not to answer a summons, they cannot do so naively, i.e. they know that if the inference of physical or interactional absence cannot be made, then some other inference will, e.g. they are cold shouldering, insulting, etc. (Schegloff 1972, pp. 367–8)

The summons–answer pair is an example of a sequence in which the first part implicates a particular type of response in the immediate next turn, to the extent that if no response occurs the first speaker is justified in, for example, repeating the summons. And on eliminating the possibility that the summons has not been heard, and determining that it will in fact not be answered, the summoner is justified in making further inferences regarding the recipient's availability, interest, and the like.[2] In this sense, we are not so much constrained by the rules of conversation as we are

---

[2] Schegloff (1972, p. 365) points to the telephone as an example of a technology that embodies the organization of the summons–answer pair:

In this mechanical age it may be of interest to note that the very construction and operation of the mechanical ring is built on these principles. If each ring of the phone be considered a summons, then the phone is built to ring, wait for an answer, if none occurs, to ring again, wait for an answer, ring again, etc. And indeed, some persons, polite even when interacting with a machine, will not interrupt a phone, but wait for the completion of a ring before picking up the receiver.

"caught in a web of inferences" (Levinson 1983, p. 321, note 16). That is to say, the rules of conversation are neither strictly optional (their breach does have consequences) nor obligatory (they may be breached without a necessary loss of coherence). They are however, inexorably meaningful.

While conditional relevance is a constraint on inference, it is a weak constraint in the sense that it does not prescribe what counts as a response to a given action, only that whatever is done next will be viewed as a response. In fact, the range of actions in a second-part position that can be heard as a response is extended in virtue of the expectation that adjacency sets up, rather than constrained. That is to say, an action that is not in any explicit way tied to the action that it follows will nevertheless be interpreted as a response, in virtue of its position:

A: Are you coming?
B: I gotta work.   (Goffman 1975, p. 260)

The position of B's utterance as a response means that we look for its relevance to A's question. So in this case, B's statement can be heard as a negative reply, just as B's question can be heard as an affirmative reply in the following:

C: Do you have coffee to go?
S: Cream and sugar?   (Merritt 1977, p. 325)

The sequential implicature exemplified by adjacency pairs is not literally conditional on adjacency, but instead allows for multiple levels of embedded sequences aimed at clarification and elaboration. The result is that answers to later questions can precede answers to earlier ones without a loss of coherence:

B: . . . I ordered some paint from you uh a couple of weeks ago some vermilion
A: Yuh
B: And I wanted to order some more the name's Boyd
(Request 1)

A: Yes//how many tubes would you like sir
(Question 1)
B: An-U:hm (.) what's the price now eh with V.A.T. do you
   know eh
(Question 2)
A: Er I'll just work that out for you=
(Hold)
B: =Thanks
(Accept)
(10.0)
A: Three pound nineteen a tube sir
(Answer 2)
B: Three nineteen is it=
(Question 3)
A: =Yeah
(Answer 3)
B: E::h (1.0) yes u:hm ((dental click)) ((in parenthetical tone))
   e:h jus-justa think, that's what three nineteen That's for the
   large tube isn't it
(Question 4)
A: Well yeah it's the thirty seven c.c.s
(Answer 4)
B: Er, hh I'll tell you what I'll just eh eh ring you back I have to
   work out how many I'll need Sorry I did- wasn't sure of the
   price you see
(Account for no Answer 1)
A: Okay

(Levinson 1983, p. 305)

The local system of adjacency pair organization, in its canonical
form operating over two turns, can by the accumulation of first
parts (e.g. requests, questions) project an extended sequence of expected seconds like that of the last example, i.e:
(R1(Q1(Q2(Q3(Q4–A4)A3)A2)A1). As Levinson points out with
respect to this example, B's final obligation is to account for his

failure to provide an answer to Question 1, demonstrating his orientation to the "social fact" that an answer is called for. That failure, in turn, effectively constitutes B's withdrawal of Request 1, freeing A of the obligation to respond to that original request:

> What the notion of conditional relevance makes clear is that what binds the parts of adjacency pairs together is not a formation rule of the sort that would specify that a question must receive an answer if it is to count as a well-formed discourse, but the setting up of specific expectations which have to be attended to. Hence the non-occurrences of an R[equest] 1 and an A[nswer]1 in [the example] do not result in an incoherent discourse because their absences are systematically provided for. (ibid., p. 306)

The overall coherence of a conversation, in sum, is accomplished through the development and elaboration of a local coherence operating in the first instance across just two turns, current and next. The resiliency of embedding, however, is such that the backward reach of relevance extends beyond the immediately preceding turn:

C: (telephone rings)
A: Hello.
C: Is this the Y?
A: You have the wrong number.
C: Is this KI five, double four, double o?
A: Double four, double *six*.
C: Oh, I am sorry.   (Goffman 1975, p. 285)

In this case the apology is intelligible only if we view the entire telephone call as its object, not just the utterance of A that it immediately follows. Similarly, to use another example of Goffman's (ibid., p. 286), the applause at the end of a play is a response not to the delivery of the final line, or the drop of the curtain, but to the entire play. The relevance of an action, in other words, is conditional on any identifiable prior action or event, however far that may extend for the participants (i.e. it may be a lifetime, say, for mother and child), insofar as the previous action can be tied to the current action's immediate, local environment. As a consequence, conditional relevance does not allow us to predict from an action to a response, but only to project that what comes next will be a response and, retrospectively, to take that status as a cue to how what comes next should be heard. The interpretation of action, in this sense, relies upon the liberal application of *post hoc, ergo propter hoc*.

5.3 Locating and remedying communicative trouble

Communication takes place in real environments, under real "performance" requirements on actual individuals, and is vulnerable therefore to internal and external troubles that may arise at any time, from a misunderstanding to a clap of thunder (Schegloff 1982). Our communication succeeds in the face of such disturbances not because we predict reliably what will happen and thereby avoid problems, or even because we encounter problems that we have anticipated in advance, but because we work, moment by moment, to identify and remedy the inevitable troubles that arise:

> It is a major feature of a rational organization for behavior that accommodates real-worldly interests, and is not susceptible of external enforcement, that it incorporates resources and procedures for repair of its troubles into its fundamental organization. (Sacks, Schegloff, and Jefferson 1978, p. 39)

The resources for detecting and remedying problems in communication, in other words, are the same resources that support communication that is trouble free. With respect to control, for example, the contingency of conversational options for keeping and taking the floor – specifically, the fact that transitions should be accomplished at possible turn completion points and not before, and that at each possible completion point the speaker may extend his or her turn – means that gaps and overlaps can and do occur.

The extent to which conversationalists accomplish speaker transitions with a minimum of gap or overlap is the product not only of the "accurate" projection of completion points, but of the repair of routine troubles. The following is a simple example of a familiar kind of conversational repair work:

C: .hhhh aa::of course *u*nder the circumstances Dee I would
     never:: again permit im tuh see im.
D: Yeah
     (0.7)
C: tlk. Be:cuz *he* –
         [
D: Wul did'e ever git – *ma*:rried'r anything?
C: Hu::*h*?
         [
D: Did yee ever git – *ma*:rried?
C: .hhhh I have no *idea*.

                                       (cited in Atkinson and Drew 1979, p. 40)

In addition to negotiating the transfer of control, participants in conversation must be alert to the possibility of substantive troubles of interpretation. Schegloff (1982) points out that tokens such as "uh huh," commonly viewed as a signal from the listener that encourages the speaker to continue, operate as they do not simply because there is a semantic convention to the effect that such tokens claim or signal understanding, but rather because through such tokens listeners pass up, at possible transition places, the opportunity to initiate repair on the preceding talk. The same option that provides for ordinary turn transitions, in other words, affords the recipient of an utterance the occasion to assert that he or she has some trouble in understanding, or to request some clarification.

The work of repair includes calling the other's attention to the occurrence of some troublesome item, remedying it, and resuming the original line of action in which the troublesome item is embedded. Jefferson (1972) identifies two kinds of trouble flag: a questioning repeat, and a non-specific interrogative, e.g. "What?" or

"Huh?" The two are different in that the repeat simultaneously flags the fact that there is some troublesome item in the prior talk, *and locates it* for the first speaker:

> Steven: One, two, three, ((pause)) four, five, six, ((pause))
> eleven, eight, nine, ten.
> Susan: "Eleven"? – eight, nine, ten?   (p. 295)

An interrogative request for clarification, in contrast, leaves it to the first speaker both to locate the item that produced the request, and to remedy it. In that case, the location of the item and the remedy may be effected simultaneously, in the first speaker's reply:

> A: If Percy goes with – Nixon I'd sure like that.
> B: *Who?*
> A: Percy.   (p. 296)

In both cases, the adjacency of the trouble flag to the troublesome item is obviously a resource for the latter's identification[3] On the other hand, listeners generally do not interrupt a speaker to flag some trouble, but rather wait for the next turn transition place, or point of completion. By permitting the speaker to complete the utterance in which the trouble is heard, the listener is warranted in assuming that there is no unsolicited remedy forthcoming, and the complaint becomes a legitimate one (p. 298).

A side sequence initiated by an assertion of misunderstanding or request for clarification sets up an exchange that the first speaker did not necessarily anticipate, but to which he or she is obliged to respond. That is to say, a failure on the part of the speaker to provide clarification in response to an explicit request is a *noticeable absence*, is seen as specifically not providing clarification, as opposed to just doing something else. The "failure to respond" then becomes something about which complaints can be made, or inferences may be drawn (Atkinson and Drew 1979, p. 57).

[3] It is worth noting in this case that while the "Who?" is in fact ambiguous, speaker A appears to have no trouble identifying its referent. It is hard to account for this in any way other than in virtue of A and B's common knowledge of politics; i.e. that it is more likely that "Percy" would be a troublesome item in this context than that "Nixon" would. Such an analysis cannot be more than conjecture, however.

In responding to a request for clarification, the sequential implicativeness of the troublesome utterance is temporarily suspended in favor of finding a remedy for the recipient's problem. Routinely in face-to-face conversation, the adjacency relation or continuity between utterance and response, and the coherence of the interaction, are sustained across such embedded side sequences. This is true even when the request for clarification results in complete reformulation of the initial utterance. That is to say, while the response may ultimately address the reformulation, not the original utterance, it will still be heard as a response to the original:

```
M:   What=so what did you do did you have people –
     did Morag(.)come(.)down with the car again( )or what
                                          [
A:                                         When last year
M:   Mmm how did you man age to shift it back and forward
          [
A:                       Last year I don't know ho:w I
     managed it I got it a::ll in (0.8) two suitcases. . .
                        (cited in Atkinson and Drew 1979, p. 239)
```

In this case it is just because A's "When last year" cannot be heard as a reply to M's question that it is heard as an embedded request for clarification. By the same token, the fact that a reply to M's question is deferred makes A's response to the reformulation about "managing it" relevant to the original question about "Morag and the car."

Turn-transition places provide recurring opportunities for the listener to initiate some repair or request for clarification from the speaker. Alternatively, clarification may be offered by the speaker not because the recipient of an utterance asks for it, but because the speaker finds evidence for some misapprehension in the recipient's response:

Dr: Hev'y ever had palpitations
     (0.6)
Pt: Noh. M' *feet* ain't painin' me but they swell sometime
Dr: No I – it's when yer heart starts beating really fast an y'feel
     like y'can't catch yer breath.
Pt: No. uh-uh. I never had th*at*   (Frankel 1984, p. 155)

While the patient here produces a response that is, formally, an answer to the doctor's question, the answer reveals a lexical problem that the doctor detects and remedies. The problem is of course unknown to the patient until the remedy is offered; if the doctor had failed to detect the misunderstanding, or had decided to let it pass and had consequently not offered the correction, the conversation to all appearances could have continued on as if there were no trouble. In this case the problem is evidently, from the doctor's point of view, worth bothering about: in myriad other cases it is not. That is to say, given the lack of specific criteria for assessing shared understanding in most cases, a crucial part of interactional competence is the ability to judge whether some evidence that the recipient has misunderstood warrants the work required for repair (Jefferson 1972). The decision whether to challenge a troublesome item or to let it pass involves, in part, a weighing of the relative work involved in the item's clarification versus the forseeable dangers of letting it go by. The risks of the latter are exemplified by the garden path situation, where speakers fail to identify some communicative trouble at the point where it occurs, and discover only at some later point in the interaction that there *has been* some misunderstanding (see Jordan and Fuller 1975, Gumperz and Tannen 1979).[4] At the point of discovery, the coherence of the interaction over some indefinite number of past turns may be called into question, and the source of the trouble may be difficult or impossible to reconstruct. In contrast to the routine problems and

[4] An instance of this in the case of human–machine communication is discussed in chapter 7, p. 171.

remedies that characterize local repair in conversation, such a situation may come close to communicative failure; that is, it may require abandoning the current line of talk, or beginning anew.

5.4 Specialized forms of interaction

A distinguishing feature of ordinary conversation is the local, moment-by-moment management of the distribution of turns, of their size, and of what gets done in them, those things being accomplished in the course of each current speaker's turn. There are, of course, numerous institutionalized settings that prescribe the organization and subject matter of interaction. Interactional organization is institutionalized along two dimensions that are of particular relevance to problems discussed in chapter 7: (1) the pre-allocation of *types* of turn, i.e. who speaks when, and what form their participation takes, and (2) the prescription of the substantive content and direction of the interaction, or the *agenda*.

5.4.1 Pre-allocation of turn types

Analysis of encounters between physicians and patients (Frankel 1984) and of the examination of witnesses in the courtroom (Atkinson and Drew 1979) reveal a turn-taking system that is pre-allocated in terms of both the types of turn, and the distribution of those types between the participants. While there is no explicit formulation of a rule for the organization of talk in medical encounters, for example, Frankel reports that physicians' utterances almost always take the form of questions (99% of the time), while patients' take the form of answers. And in the courtroom, by definition, the examiner has the sole right to ask questions, while the examined is obliged to answer. In the courtroom, the convention that only two parties participate holds in spite of the number of persons present, and with the exception only of certain prescribed methods for "interruption" from the other counsel which, in virtue of the prescription of when and how interruption is to be effected, itself becomes a technical matter in the courtroom setting. In both medical and legal settings, the effect of the pre-allocation of turn types is to deliver control of the proceedings from the "client" or layperson back to the "expert" or specialist. At the close of each question–answer sequence, control is relinquished to whoever would start another sequence and the expert, having rights to the role of questioner, is repeatedly the one to re-take control.

While the constraints on medical or legal interaction can be seen as institutional, and in that sense as external to any particular occasion, it is nonetheless the case that in every actual instance the constraints are realized locally and collaboratively. Insofar as the interaction is locally managed, turn-transitions are subject to the same problems that arise in everyday conversation, and are remedied via the same methods, as in the following example of an overlap that the witness (W) remedies by repeating her answer to the counsel's (C's) question:

```
C:    An (.) about how long did you say you
      ta:lked before (this was)
               [
W:             I don't remember
C:    (started ta kiss (h) a)=
W:    =I don't remember.
```
(from Atkinson and Drew 1979, p. 67)

At the same time, the fact that procedural constraints on turn transitions are managed locally, even in these settings, means that general conventions of conversational turn-taking can be exploited to further the special purposes of the participants. Because of the fact that pauses in conversation, for example, will be ascribed significance insofar as they are seen to belong to a selected next speaker, a pause following an examination sequence can be used by the examining counsel effectively to comment on the response to the jury, as in the following examination in a rape case cited by Atkinson and Drew (p. 241):

C: You were out in the woods with the defendant at this point
     isn't that so
     (1.0)
W: Yeah
     (7.0)
C: And the defendant (.) took (.) the ca:r (1.0) and backed
     it (1.0) into some trees didn'e
     (0.5)
W: Mm hm
          [
C: underneath some trees.

In this case, the pre-allocated order of turns assigns the 7-second
pause to the counsel – and ensures that no other speaker will use
the pause as an opportunity to take over the floor. The pause is
used by the counsel in an unspoken turn that insinuates further
"information" into the message that the jury receives from the witness's answer. In the medical encounter, similarly, the physician
can use a silence as an unspoken turn – in the following example, in
order to avoid having to deliver bad news through disagreement:

Pt: This – chemotherapy (0.2) it won't have any lasting effects
      on havin' kids will it?
      (2.2)
Pt: It will?
Dr: I'm afraid so.   (Frankel 1984, p. 153)

Finally, although respective turns of physician and patient, or
counsel and witness, are constrained to be either questions or
answers, these are minimal characterizations, and provide no
instruction for how, or what, specific utterances can be put into
such a format. In the courtroom, for example, rules of evidence
apply – relevance to the case at hand, status of the evidence as hear-
say, the use of leading questions, and the like – where the application of those rules is situated and problematic, and is itself part of

the technical business of the proceedings. And the format of questions and answers in the courtroom accommodates a range of activities including accusations, challenges, justifications, denials, and the like. Those activities are not prescribed in the way that the question–answer format is, and what counts as a question or an answer is itself liable to challenge. As a consequence, rules for courtroom interaction, like those for everyday conversation, constitute a resource for social order, not a recipe or an explanation.

5.4.2 Agendas

Various settings, of course, do comprise prescriptions not only about forms of talk, but also about the substantive direction and purposes of the interaction:

> in several different types of speech-exchange situations, there can be occasions in which participation is constructed by a speaker in continuing response to interactional contingencies and opportunities from moment to moment, and occasions in which a participant has a preformed notion, and sometimes a prespecified text, of what is to be said, and plows ahead with it in substantial (though rarely total) disregard for what is transpiring in the course of his talking. (Schegloff 1982, p. 72)

A major concern for participants in such settings is the distribution of knowledge about the agenda (Beckman and Frankel 1983). The communicative task of novice and expert in a given setting is to coordinate their actions in a way that accommodates their asymmetrical relationship to the interaction's institutionalized purposes. At the same time, it is precisely the difference in their respective familiarities *vis-à-vis* the setting's protocols and purposes that in large measure distinguishes the "expert" or specialist from the "novice" or layperson (Erickson and Shultz 1982, p. 4).

The work of Beckman and Frankel (1983) on physicians' methods for eliciting a patient's "chief complaint" is illustrative. They point out that the medical literature has generally viewed the agenda for medical interviews as the patient's, in the sense that it is the patient who comes to the physician with a complaint, and who is the source of the information required for the complaint's diagnosis. Given this view, a commonly cited problem for physicians is the experience of discovering, at the point where the physician is about to conclude the office visit or at least the history-taking segment of the interview, that the patient has withheld some information that is relevant to a chief complaint. In contrast, by inverting the common view, Beckman and Frankel identify the relevant agenda in medical encounters as the physician's, and further locate the source of the "hidden agenda" problem in ways that the *physician*'s actions, in the opening sequence of the clinical encounter, serve systematically to foreclose a complete report of symptoms by the patient.[5]

The point of Beckman and Frankel's observation that is most relevant for present purposes – a point that I return to in chapter 6 – is their insight that analysts of the medical interview have been misconceiving the essential problem for the interaction. Specifically, the problem is not that the patient "hides" the agenda, but that the patient, as a novice in this setting, does not understand the institutional purposes of the interaction, i.e. the identification of a "chief complaint," or the physician's strategy for achieving those purposes. The patient's task is misconceived, therefore, if it is viewed as either carrying out the plan of the interview, or as failing to do so. The point is rather that the patient *does not know the plan*, and is therefore able to cooperate only to the extent that being responsive to the physician's actions, locally, constitutes cooperation in realizing the plan. To the extent that the patient's cooperation is contingent on the physician's actions, the success of the interview is as well.

---

[5] Specifically, they cite the physician's tendency, given any mention of symptoms by the patient, to engage in early hypothesis testing: "once hypothesis testing has begun, it is difficult for the patient to get a word in edgewise without deviating from conventional rules of discourse which relate types of speech acts to one another, in this case the relevance of an answer to the question that preceded it" (p. 9).

The actual production of an agenda, through local interactional work, is evident in the following excerpt from a career counseling interview, reported by Erickson and Shultz (1982, pp. 77–8); C = counselor, S = student):

C: Well, let's start from scratch. What did you get in your English 100 last semester?

S: A "C."

C: Biology 101?

S: "A."

C: Reading 100?

S: "B."

C: Med tech. . .'B'? (medical technology)

S: "B."

C: Gym?

S: "A."

C: Was that a full credit hour? What was it?

S: It was a wrestling. . .two periods.

C: Wrestling. (He writes this on the record card, then shifts postural position and looks up from the record at the student.) Ok, this semester. . .English 101?

S: (Changes facial expression, but no nod or "mhm" in response to the question.)

C: That's what you've got now. . .

S: (Nods.)

C: Biology 102? Soc Sci 101. (The counselor is looking down.)

S: I. . .I. . .don't have Biology 102. I have, mm, 112.

C: (The counselor corrects the record card.) Soc Sci 101?

S: (Nods.) Mhm.

C: Math 95.

S: (Nods.)

C: Med Tech 112.

S: (Nods.)

C: Gym.

S: (Nods.)

In Erickson and Shultz's analysis, this interview comprises two adjacent routines, by which the counselor establishes the student's academic status first as a matter of courses completed, and then as a matter of courses underway. The problem negotiated by counselor and student is that the counselor's behavior is superficially the same across both routines, so that the juncture or transition between them, which requires a change in the task of the student, is initially missed by the student. The student's failure to respond to the query "English 101?" demonstrates the problem to the counselor, who then offers a remedy.

While the organization of this and any interaction can be analyzed *post hoc* into a hierarchical structure of topics and subtopics, or routines and subroutines, the coherence that the structure represents is actually achieved moment by moment, as a local, collaborative, sequential accomplishment. This observation stands in marked contrast to the assumptions of students of discourse to the effect that the actual enactment of interaction is the behavioral realization of a plan. Instead, every instance of coherent interaction is an essentially local production, accomplished collaboratively in real time, rather than "born naturally whole out of the speaker's forehead, the delivery of a cognitive plan" (Schegloff 1982, p. 73):

> Good analysis retains a sense of the actual as an achievement from among possibilities; it retains a lively sense of the contingency of real things. It is worth an alert, therefore, that too easy a notion of "discourse" can lose us that. . .

If certain stable forms appear to emerge or recur in talk, they should be understood as an orderliness wrested by the participants from interactional contingency, rather than as automatic products of standardized plans. Form, one might say, is also the distillate of action and interaction, not only its blueprint. If that is so, then the description of forms of behavior, forms of discourse... included, has to include interaction among their constitutive domains, and not just as the stage on which scripts written in the mind are played out. (ibid., p. 89)

The organization of face-to-face interaction is the paradigm case of a system that has evolved in the service of orderly, concerted action over an indefinite range of essentially unpredictable circumstances. What is notable about that system is the extent to which mastery of its constraints localizes and thereby leaves open questions of control and direction, while providing built-in mechanisms for recovery from trouble and error. The constraints on interaction in this sense are not determinants of, but are rather "production resources" (Erickson 1982) for, shared understanding. The limits on available resources for accomplishing a shared agenda in a case of "interaction" between people and machines, and for detecting and remedying the troubles that that task poses, is the subject of chapter 7.

Notation

[Bracket indicates a point at which a current speaker's talk is overlapped by the talk of another, with overlapping talk directly beneath.

//   Alternatively, double oblique lines indicate point at which current speaker's talk is overlapped by the talk of a next speaker.

:   Colons indicate a lengthened syllable, the number of colons corresponding to the extent of lengthening.

–   Dash indicates stop, cutting off an utterance.

?   Question intonation.

.   Full stop, with falling intonation.

=   Equals sign indicates no interval between the end of a prior and the start of a next piece of talk.

.hh   Audible breath. Dot before indicates inbreath, no dot indicates outbreath.

italics   Speaker's emphasis.

( )   Words enclosed in parenthesis indicate either non-linguistic action, or transcriber's uncertainty over verbatim.

(( ))   Double parenthesis indicates features of the audio other than verbalization, or note from the transcriber.

Notation

(0.0)   Numbers in parenthesis indicate elapsed time in tenths of a second.

(.)   Untimed pause.

For a more extensive description of notations see Jefferson 1983, Heritage 1984 and Lynch 1985.

6 Case and methods

In this age, in which social critics complain about the replacement of men by machines, this small corner of the social world has not been uninvaded. It is possible, nowadays, to hear the phone you are calling picked up and hear a human voice answer, but nevertheless not be talking to a human. However small its measure of consolation, we may note that even machines such as the automatic answering device are constructed on social, and not only mechanical, principles. The machine's magnetic voice will not only answer the caller's ring, but will also inform him when its ears will be available to receive his message, and warn him both to wait for the beep and confine his interests to fifteen seconds. (Shegloff 1972, p. 374)

Chapter 7 describes people's first encounters with a machine called an *expert help system*: a computer-based system attached to a large and relatively complex photocopier, and intended to instruct the user of the copier in its operation.[1] The system's identification as an "expert help system" both locates it in the wider category of so-called expert systems, and indicates that a function of this system is to provide procedural instructions to the user. The idea of expert systems in general is that expertise consists in a body of propositions or "knowledge" about a particular domain, and rules for its use. The knowledge of this system comprises a set of rules about copying jobs and procedures that control both the presentation of

[1] The system was designed by Richard Fikes at the Xerox Palo Alto Research Center in 1982–3.

instructions to the user on a video display and the operations of the copier itself. The design objective is that the system should provide timely and relevant information to the user regarding the operation of the copier. The information should be presented not as a compendium, but in a step-wise order wherein each next instruction is invoked by the user's successful enactment of the last. To provide the user with appropriate instruction, therefore, the system must somehow recognize the action of the user to which it should respond. It is this problem in particular, the problem of the system's recognition of the user's actions, that the analysis explores.

6.1 The expert help system

In contrast to relatively unrestricted occasions of human interaction such as ordinary conversation, certain constraints on the event of using the expert help system provide grounds for imagining that one might safely predict, in some detail, just how the event will go:

- The interaction is instrumental;
- The possible goals of the interaction are defined by the machine's functionality;
- The structure of the interaction is procedural, constituted by a sequence of actions whose order is partially enforced;
- The criteria of adequacy for each action can be specified.

Because in machine operation the user's purposes are constrained by the machine's functionality, and her actions by its design, it seems reasonable to suppose that the user's purposes should serve as a sufficient context for the interpretation of her actions. On this assumption, the strategy that the design adopts is to project the course of the user's actions as the enactment of a plan for doing the job, and then use the presumed plan as the relevant context for the action's interpretation.[2] Through the user's response to a series of

[2] As chapter 3 pointed out, analysts of the intention–action relationship are troubled by the apparently diffuse and tacit nature of intentions in many situations, and the

questions about the state of her original documents and the desired copies, her purposes are identified with a job specification, the specification (represented in the system as a data structure with variable fields) invokes an associated plan, and the enactment of the plan is prescribed by the system as a step-wise procedure.

Having mapped the user's purposes to a job specification, and the job specification to a plan, the plan is then effectively ascribed to the user as the basis for interpreting her actions. The rationale for this move is that the plan is conveyed to the user in the form of instructions for a step-wise procedure, the user is following the instructions and consequently, one can assume, is following the plan that the instructions describe. Under that assumption, the effects of certain actions by the user are mapped to a place in the system's plan, and that mapping is used to locate an appropriate next instruction. The actions by the user that effect changes in the machine's state comprise some physical actions on the machine (putting documents into document trays, opening and closing machine covers and the like), and directives to the system in the form of selections of text on a video display. The hope of the designer is that the effects of these actions by the user can be mapped reliably to a location in the system's plan, and that the location in the plan will determine an appropriate system response. The relevant sense of "interaction" in this case, therefore, is that the provision of instruction is both fitted to the user's purposes and occasioned by her actions.

The design assumes, however, that it is the correspondence of the system's plan to the user's purposes that enables the interaction. In contrast, the analysis of chapter 7 indicates that user and

consequent problem of determining just what is the actor's "true" intent. This seems less of a problem with goal-directed activities, where the goal, as defined by the analyst, can simply be taken *a priori* as the intent of the actor. The argument of this book, of course, is that the relief from the problem of determining intent that task-oriented interaction seems to offer is only a temporary palliative to the designer's problem; the real solution must lie in an alternative understanding of the nature of intentions and their relation to actions – one that views the everyday business of identifying intent as an essentially contingent, practical, and interactional accomplishment.

system each have a consequentially different relationship to the design plan. While the plan directly determines the system's behavior, the user is required to find the plan, as the prescriptive and descriptive significance of a series of procedural instructions. While the instructions, and the procedure that they describe, are the object of the user's work, they do not reconstruct the work's course, nor do they determine its outcome.

6.2 *The problem of following instructions*

The practical problem that the expert help system was designed to solve arises out of the work of following instructions, which in turn leads to the work of communicating them. The general task in following instructions is to bring canonical descriptions of objects and actions to bear on the actual objects and embodied actions that the instructions describe (Lynch, Livingston, and Garfinkel 1983). Studies of instruction in cognitive and social science alike have focused, on the one hand, on the problem of providing adequate instructions and, on the other, on the problem of finding the practical significance of instructions for situated action.

Social studies of the production and use of instructions have concentrated on the irremediable incompleteness of instructions (Garfinkel 1967, ch. 1), and the nature of the work required in order to "carry them out." The problem of the instruction-follower is viewed as one of turning essentially partial descriptions of objects and actions into concrete practical activities with predictable outcomes (Zimmerman 1970; Amerine and Bilmes 1979). A general observation from these studies is that instructions rely upon the recipient's ability to do the implicit work of anchoring descriptions to concrete objects and actions. At the same time, that work remains largely unexamined by either instruction-writer or recipient, particularly when the work goes smoothly.

In a study of instruction-following as practical action, Amerine and Bilmes (1979) point out that instructions serve not only as prescriptions for what to do, but also as resources for retrospective accounts of what has happened:

> Successfully following instructions can be described as constructing a course of action such that, having done this course of action, the instructions will serve as a descriptive account of what has been done. (p. 5)

More than the "correct" execution of an instruction, in other words, successful instruction-following is a matter of constructing a particular course of action that is accountable to the general description that the instruction provides. The work of constructing that course is neither exhaustively enumerated in the description, nor completely captured by a retrospective account of what was done. Instructions serve as a resource for describing what was done not only because they guide the course of action, but also because they filter out of the retrospective account of the action, or treat as "noise," everything that was actually done that the instructions fail to mention:

> If the experiment is "successful", if it achieves its projected outcome, the instructions can serve as an account of "what was done," although in the actual performance a great deal more is necessarily done than can be comprised in the instructions. (p. 3)

The credibility of instructions, moreover, rests on the premise that not only do they describe what action to take, but that if they are followed correctly the action will produce a predictable outcome. An unexpected outcome, accordingly, indicates trouble and warrants some remedy. As long as instructions are viewed as authoritative, the preference in remedying a faulted outcome is to account for the failure in outcome without discrediting the instruction. An obvious solution is to locate the trouble somewhere in the instruction's "execution." In assessing the course of the work for troubles in execution, questions inevitably arise concerning the relation of the many actions that were taken that are not specified by the instructions, to the faulted outcome. Previously insignificant details may appear crucial, or the meaning of the instructions may be transformed in such a way that they are found not to have been followed after all. Amerine and Bilmes give an example, drawn from science experiments in a third-grade classroom, of the kind of problem inherent in reasoning inductively about the relation between courses of action and outcomes:

> To expedite carrying out this lesson two similar and functionally equivalent pans of water were placed on a table in the center of the room and the students were called on by pairs to try the exercise. Toward that end, when, as related above, this activity had become particularly competitive, one of the children approached a pan but was urged by classmates to use the other one because it was "luckier." We are not sure how this notion came about, although in a pair of trials closely preceding this comment the student using the "unlucky" pan had failed, while the child using the other one had succeeded. At any rate, the student followed this advice and the experiment was successful. Both of the following two children rushed for the "lucky" pan, though the loser settled for the "unlucky" one (and succeeded nonetheless). In the case of the next pair, the second child waited for the first to finish using the "lucky" pan, and then also used it. The "unlucky" pan remained unused thereafter . . . In neither case are such observations by *nature* illogical or irrelevant . . . But in these science experiments our understanding of the relationship between the practical course of action and its outcome seems to leave no place for "luck" . . . Therefore such factors become "noise." (pp. 9–10, original emphasis)

The ability to discriminate between relevant information and "noise" in a given domain of action, by invoking both precepts and practice, is a part of what we recognize as expertise. The point of the "lucky pan" examples is that the process by which that ability is acquired is a fundamentally inductive and *ad hoc* one, regardless of the degree to which rules of action are encoded and prescribed. In the final analysis, no amount of prescription, however precise or elaborate, can relieve situated action "of the burden of finding a way through an unscheduled future while making a convincing case for what is 'somehow' extracted from that future" (Lynch, Livingston, and Garfinkel 1983, p. 233). The latter is the problem of accountably rational, situated action, however adequate the instructions for that action may be.

6.3 Communicating instructions

An appreciation for what is required in instruction-following makes it easier to understand the problem that the communication of instructions attempts to solve: namely, the troubles inherent in turning an instruction into an action. Motivated by the project of designing instructional computer systems, researchers in artificial intelligence have looked at instruction as a question of communicative resources available to expert and novice. One of the earliest such projects, the Computer-Based Consultant project begun at Stanford Research Institute in the 1970s, continues to direct research on task-oriented communication through "natural language," using what has become the canonical problem of assembling a simple mechanical device. The goal of the original project was:

> to produce a computer system that could fill the role of an expert in the cooperative execution of complex tasks with a relatively inexperienced human apprentice. The system was to use rich channels of communication, including natural language and eventually speech. The main function of the consultant was to aid the apprentice in the diagnosis of faulty electromechanical equipment, and the formulation of plans for the assembly, disassembly, and repair of the equipment. (Sacerdoti 1977, p. 3)

Using an air compressor as the assembly task, researchers collected a corpus of dialogues in experiments designed to simulate inter-action between a person and a computer (Grosz 1981). In these experiments two people – one acting as expert, and the other acting as apprentice – had only limited visual access to each other. Grosz's analysis of the corpus turns on the observation that the require-ment for successful communication between expert and novice, despite their limited visual access, is a common "focus" on the task at hand. Common focus allows the exploitation of language (e.g. definite descriptions such as "the screw"), materials ("the screw visible on the hub of the flywheel"), and local history ("the screw loosened previously") in instruction, while language, materials, and history are used, in turn, to maintain the common focus. Grosz's concern with the linguistic, interactional, and material bases of successful instruction set the stage for a series of sub-sequent analyses in which, by varying the resources available for communication, researchers began to explore the relationship of various non-linguistic resources to the use of language (for a "tax-onomy" of these resources, see Rubin 1980).

In an analysis of transcripts of instructors communicating with an apprentice through face-to-face, telephone, audio-taped, and written media about the assembly of a toy water pump, Burke (1982) found that the most obvious difference, that between speak-ing and writing, is actually less crucial than the difference between interactive (e.g. a keyboard) and non-interactive (e.g. audio-taped) instruction. The restrictions generally associated with written instruction, in other words, derive not from the writing so much as from the absence of interaction, while the effectiveness of verbal instruction derives less from the speech than from the interaction that is generally associated with it.

Ochs (1979) relates the distinction of interactive and non-interactive communication to degrees of planning, arguing that in the case of interaction, speakers plan only at a general level (the concretization of the plan being contingent and emergent), where-as non-interactive discourse can be entirely planned in advance. Instead, Burke takes the point of view that the instructor's task is one of adequate description rather than planning, and reports that in the non-interactive modalities of instruction on the assembly task there is a tendency to "overelaborate" descriptions, in an apparent attempt to anticipate possible troubles, and to compensate for the lack of opportunities for their on-site clarification. In face-to-face instruction, in contrast, Burke found that instructors initially provided minimal descriptions, and then monitored the apprentice's actions for evidence of the description's adequacy or inadequacy. By telephone, where visual access was unavailable, but where the interaction remained, the resources for monitoring the actions of the apprentice changed from visual to verbal (e.g. affirmations, repeats, and transformed repeats of the instructions by the apprentice), but the monitoring again guided the description.

Cohen's (n.d.) analysis of transcripts of instructor and apprentice communicating by telephone or keyboard on the same assembly task confirms the ability of instructors to adjust the level of their descriptions in response to the demonstrated understanding or misunderstanding by the apprentice. He concludes that the principal difference between spoken and written interactive media is that experts in spoken instruction more often explicitly request that the novice identify an object, and often question the novice on his or her success, while experts using keyboards subsume reference to objects into instructions for action unless some prior referential miscommunication has occurred (p. 21). Spoken interaction between expert and novice, in that sense, is more finely calibrated than written, though insofar as both are interactive, both support the collaborative construction of a "useful description" of the objects and actions in question, through practical analyses of the communication's success at each turn.

6.4 The basic interaction

The aim of the expert help system analyzed in the next chapter is to use the power of the computer to combine the portability of non-interactive instructions, with the timeliness, relevance, and effectiveness of interaction. The machine presents the user with a series of video displays. Each display presented to the user either describes the machine's behavior, or provides the user with some next instructions. In the latter case, the final instruction of each display prescribes an action whose effect is detectable by the system, thereby triggering a change to the next display.

1. MACHINE PRESENTS INSTRUCTION

   User reads instruction
   interprets referents
   and action descriptions

2. USER TAKES ACTION

   Design assumes
   that the action means
   that the user has understood
   the instruction

3. MACHINE PRESENTS NEXT INSTRUCTION

THE BASIC INSTRUCTIONAL SEQUENCE

Through the device of display changes keyed to actions by the user, the design accomplishes a simple form of occasioned response, in spite of the fact that only a partial trace of the user's behavior is available to the system. Among those user actions that are *not* available to the system is the actual work of locating referents and interpreting action descriptions: the system has access only to the product of that work. Moreover, within the instruction provided by a given display are embedded instructions for actions whose effects are not detectable by the system. To anticipate our discussion of troubles that arise, if one of *these* instructions is misconstrued, the error will go by unnoticed. Since the implication of a next display is that prior actions have been noted, and that they have been found adequate, the appearance of a next instruction will confirm the correctness not only of the prior action narrowly defined, but of all the embedded actions prescribed by the last instruction.

To compensate for the machine's limited access to the user's actions, the design relies upon a partial enforcement of the order of user actions within the procedural sequence. This strategy works fairly well, insofar as a particular effect produced by the user (such as closing a cover on the copier) can be taken to imply that a certain condition obtains (a document has been placed in the machine for copying) which, in turn, implies a machine response (the initiation of the printing process). In this sense, the order of user and machine "turns," and what is to be accomplished in each, is predetermined. The system's "recognition" of turn-transition places is essentially reactive; that is, there is a determinate relationship between certain uninterpreted actions by the user, read as changes to the state of the machine, and the machine's transition to a next display. By establishing a determinate relationship between detectable user actions and machine responses, the design unilaterally administers control over the interaction, but in a way that is conditional on the actions of the user.

At the same time that the system controls the sequence of user actions, the design avoids certain problems that arise when instructions are provided consecutively and in a strict order. Every procedure is represented in the system as a series of steps, each of which has an associated precondition (the effect of a prior action by user or machine), and an associated machine response (display of instructions and/or setting of machine state). Rather than proceeding through these steps consecutively, the system begins processing at the *last* step of the procedure and checks to see whether that step has been completed. If not, the preconditions are checked and, if they are all satisfied, the step is executed. Each precondition carries with it a reference to the earlier step in the procedure that will satisfy that precondition, so that if an unmet precondition is found the system will return to the earlier step, and proceed from there. If, therefore, a procedure is repeated, but in the second instance certain conditions hold over from the first, the system will not display instructions for the actions that have already been taken. Beginning with the final step, it will work backwards through the procedure just to the point where an unmet precondition is found, and will provide the instruction from that point on. Similarly, if the user takes an action that undoes a condition satisfied earlier, the system will encounter that state again at the next check. This technique produces appropriate instructions not because the system knows that this time through differs from the last, but just because, regardless of how they come about, certain detectable conditions (e.g. a document is in the machine) are linked unequivocally to appropriate response (e.g. initiating the printing process). Chapter 7 examines how this design strategy works and how, for the very same reason that it works in some instances, in other instances troubles arise.

6.4 Methods

The study was directed by two methodological commitments, one general, the other particular to the problem at hand.

Generally, the study began with a commitment to an empirical approach, along with the conviction that situated action cannot be captured empirically through either examples constructed by the researcher, paper and pencil observations, or interview reports. Analyses of contrived examples, observations, or interviews all rest upon accounts of circumstances that are either imagined or recollected. One objective in studying situated action is to consider just those fleeting circumstances that our interpretations of action systematically rely upon, but which our accounts of action routinely ignore. A second objective is to make the relation between interpretations of action and action's circumstances our subject matter. Both objectives are clearly lost if we use reports of action as our data.[3]

Another approach to the analysis of instructions might be to look at the textual cogency of the instructions themselves. An example offered by Searle (1979) illustrates the problem with such a strategy:[4]

> Suppose a man goes to the supermarket with a shopping list given him by his wife on which are written the words "beans, butter, bacon, and bread." Suppose as he goes around with his shopping cart selecting these items, he is followed by a detective who writes down everything he takes. As they emerge from the store both the shopper and detective will have identical lists. But the function of the two lists will be quite different. In the case of the shopper's list, the purpose of the list is, so to speak, to get the world to match the words; the man is supposed to make his actions fit the list. In the case of the detective, the purpose of the list is to make the words match the world; the man is supposed to make the list fit the actions of the shopper. This can be fur-

[3] This is not to say that paper and pencil observations do not have their place. The video analysis was preceded by approximately twenty hours of observation of new users of the same machine, minus the "expert help system" but equipped with written instructions, in actual office settings. That earlier study was undertaken in response to an unelaborated report, from those who supported the machine and its users "in the field," of user complaints that the machine was too complicated. Given the relative simplicity of even the most complex photocopier, this complaint on face value was puzzling, particularly to the machine's designers. The combination of the vagueness of the complaint as reported, and the bewilderment of the designers, intrigued both me and my colleagues Austin Henderson and Richard Fikes at the research center, and we set about to try to ascertain what the "complexity" was really about. That led to the paper and pencil observations, which convinced us that indeed the machine *was* somehow too complicated for the novice user who had no previous training; that is, people trying to use the machine were visibly confused. The methodological problem at that point was that I, as an observer of their troubles, was equally confused. From the observations, therefore, I learned two important lessons. First, that there was indeed a problem. And secondly, that to understand the problem would require the use of an adequate, i.e. a videotaped, record. For an analysis of users' troubles with the original instruction set, see Suchman 1982.

[4] Searle credits this example to Anscombe (1957). The point that Searle is interested in concerns the notion of "direction of fit" between words and the world.

ther demonstrated by observing the role of "mistake" in the two cases. If the detective goes home and suddenly realizes that the man bought pork chops instead of bacon, he can simply erase the word "bacon" and write "pork chops." But if the shopper gets home and his wife points out that he has bought pork chops when he should have bought bacon he cannot correct the mistake by erasing "bacon" from the list and writing "pork chops." (p. 4)

The subject of the present analysis, the user of the expert help system, is in the position of the shopper with respect to the instructions that the system provides; that is, she must make her actions match the words. But in what sense? Like the instructions, a shopping list may be consulted to decide what to do next or to know when the shopping is done, may be cited after the fact to explain why things were done the way they were, and so forth. But also like the instructions, the list does not actually describe the practical activity of shopping (how to find things, which aisles to go down in what order, how to decide between competing brands, etc.); it simply says how that activity is to turn out.

Just as the list of the shopping's outcomes does not actually describe the organization of the activity of shopping, an analysis of instructions will not yield an analysis of the activity of carrying them out. In fact, contrary to the case in the story, there is no reason to believe that if a person has a set of instructions for operating a machine, and we generate a description of the activity of operating a machine from watching the person, that the description we generate should look anything like the instructions. In fact, if our description of the situated activity does mirror the structure of the instructions, there is reason to believe that something is amiss.

Unlike the detective in the story who is supposed to generate a list, our problem as students of situated action is more akin to the problem of a detective who is just sent out and told to report back on what going to the grocery store is all about and how it is done. What that description should look like – what its terms should be, what its structure should be, what of all that goes on it should report – is an open methodological question. If, in order to put some constraints on the description, we set out with a template that asks for a list just of what the actions come to, then what counts as "an action" is prescribed ahead of time as "its outcome," and the list format prescribes the structure of the description. Only that part of the activity that fills in the template will be recorded. The action's structure, in other words, will be decided in advance, and the method employed by the scientist will ensure that that structure is what is found.

One further issue that the story touches on is the problem of validity. The story says the detective might "suddenly realize" that there is some error in his description. But how might he actually realize that? If we just look for a discrepancy between the shopper's list and the detective's, what we find might reflect either an error in the shopper's activity (it doesn't match the list) or in the description (it doesn't match the activity). In order to evaluate which, we must have (a) independent access to the shopper's list, to compare against the activity; and (b) a record of activity. That is to say, two essential, methodological resources are (a) the comparison of our own interpretations with those of our subjects, and (b) a record that is not contingent on either.

However adequate the record, of course, the empiricism of social studies is not a positive one because we cannot, by definition, provide a literal description of our phenomenon.[5] As Wilson (1970) defines literal description:

> Any description of a phenomenon is based on perceived features that the phenomenon displays to the observer. A literal description, then, amounts to asserting that on the basis of

---

[5] Galaty (1981) makes a useful distinction between "data sources," as the business of the social world independent of the anthropologist's interest in it; "data," as the anthropologically processed information that appears in the form of, for example, transcripts; and "analytic objects," conceptualized as events, troubles, and the like (note 2, p. 91). The point is that for the social scientist, the data are interpreted already at its source.

those features the phenomenon has some clearly designated property, or what is logically the same thing, belongs to some particular, well-defined class of phenomena. (p. 72)

In order for a description to be literal, in other words, the class of phenomena of which the described is an instance must be definable in terms of sufficient conditions for counting some instance as a member of the class. For situated action, that would require classification of action not only as the relation of intent to behavior, but as the relation of both to mitigating circumstances – a classification which, I argued in chapter 4, is functionally and criterially different from that applied to intentional descriptions of actions and situations. Moreover, the social scientist's description is yet another order of remove from a literal description if the subject of the description is not only the intent of some actor, but the interpretations of that actor's intent by others on the scene. Judgments of correctness and veridicality are replaced in social studies by judgments of adequacy or verisimilarity (Heap 1980, p. 104), the latter resting on criteria of evidence and warranted inference, rather than conditions of truth.

The problems that the social scientist struggles with in defining her methods are the same problem that, from another view, constitute her subject matter: namely, the uncertain relation between accounts of the significance of action, and the observations and inferences on which those accounts must be based. There is no privileged analytic stance for the social scientist that exempts her from the problems of adjudicating the practical objectivity of the social world. The only advantage that accrues to the researcher (a substantial one, it turns out) is recourse to a record of the action and its circumstances, independent of her analysis. The availability of audiovisual technology that can provide such a record, for repeated inspection by the researcher and by colleagues, avoids the reliance on unexplicated resources that characterizes traditional ethnographic accounts. In traditional accounts, the fleeting nature of the events that the ethnographer describes means that the only record that is available for inspection by others is the ethnographer's description.

This study proceeded, therefore, in a setting where video technology could be used in a sort of uncontrolled experimentation. On the one hand, the situation was constructed so as to make certain issues observable – specifically, the work of using the machine with the assistance of the expert help system. The construction consisted in the selection of tasks observed to pose problems for new users in "the real world." On the other hand, once given those tasks, the subjects were left entirely on their own. In the analysis, by the same token, the goal was to construct a characterization of the "interaction" that ensued, rather than to apply a predetermined coding scheme. Both predetermined coding schemes and controlled experiments presuppose a characterization of the phenomenon studied, varying only certain parameters to test the characterization. Application of that methodology to the problem of human–machine interaction would be at the least premature. The point of departure for the study was the assumption that we *lack* a description of the structure of situated action. And because the hunch is that the structure lies in a relation between action and its circumstances that we have yet to uncover, we do not want to *presuppose* what are the relevant conditions, or their relationship to the structure of the action. We need to begin, therefore, at the beginning, with observations that capture as much of the phenomenon, and presuppose as little, as possible.

The consequence of this commitment to examining the circumstances of action is that we need to begin with a record of events which is not pre-judged as to its analytic interest either in advance or in the making. The data for this study, accordingly, are a corpus of videotapes of first-time users of the expert help system.[6] First-time users were chosen on the grounds that the system was intended by its designers to be self-explanatory, or usable by people with no previous introduction to the machine. More generally, the troubles encountered by first-time users of a system are valuable in

[6] The corpus includes four sessions, each lasting from one and a half to two hours.

that they disclose work required to understand the system's behavior that, for various reasons, is masked by the proficient user. This disclosure of the requisite work is the value of studying interactional *troubles* generally (see Gumperz 1982b, p. 308), and distinguishes this analysis from the usual "operability tests." That is to say, I am not simply interested in distinguishing "correct" from "erroneous" moves by the user. Rather, by studying what things look like when they are unfamiliar and troublesome, I hope to understand better what is involved in their mastery.

In each of the sessions two people, neither of whom had ever used the system before, worked together in pairs. Two people asked to collaborate in using a relatively simple machine like a photocopier are faced with the problem of doing together what either could do alone. In the interest of the collaboration, each makes available to the other what she believes to be going on: what the task is, how it is to be accomplished, what has already been done and what remains, rationales for this way of proceeding over that, and so forth. Through the ways in which each collaborator works to provide her sense of what is going on to the other, she provides that sense to the researcher as well. An artifact of such a collaboration, therefore, is naturally generated protocol.[7]

A second methodological commitment, which arose from the particular problem of looking at human–machine communication, directed the analysis itself. The aim of the analysis was to find the sense of "shared understanding" in human–machine communication. More particularly, I wanted to compare the user's and the system's respective views of the interaction, over a sequence of

---

[7] Brown, Rubenstein, and Burton (1976) argue persuasively for the use of teams to generate protocols, where the discussions and arguments that unfold are treated as evidence for the individual reasoning of the participants. The actions of the team members can also be viewed as organized by the task of collaboration itself, however, although in the interest of looking at the interaction of both users with the machine, I have deliberately avoided taking that view here. It is worth noting, in this regard, that analyses of "discourse" undertaken in the interest of building interactive AI systems generally tend to view communication as the coincidence of individual reasoning processes, rather than as an activity with a distinctive character arising from the collaboration itself.

events. In working to organize the transcripts of the videotapes, therefore, I arrived at the following simple framework:

THE USER		THE MACHINE	
Actions not available to the machine	Actions available to the machine	Effects available to the user	Design rationale

THE ANALYTIC FRAMEWORK

The framework revealed two initial facts about the relationship of user and system. First, it showed that the coherence of the user's actions was largely unavailable to the system, and something of why that was the case. Beginning with the observation that what the user was trying to do was, somehow, available to me as the researcher, I could ask how that was so. The richest source of information for the researcher, as a fully fledged, "intelligent" observer, is the verbal protocol (recorded in the first column). In reading the instructions aloud, the user locates the problem that she is working on. Her questions about the instructions identify the problem more particularly, and further talk provides her interpretations of the machine's behavior, and clarifies her actions in response.

A second, but equally crucial resource is visual access to the user's actions. Of all of her actions, one could clearly see the very small subset, recorded in the second column, that were actually detected by the system. From the system's "point of view," correspondingly, one could see how it was that those traces of the user's actions available to the system – the user's behavior seen, as it were, through a key-hole – were mapped onto the system's plan, under the design assumption that, for example, button x pushed at this particular point in the procedure must mean that the user is doing y.

The framework proved invaluable for taking seriously the idea that user and machine were interacting. By treating the center two columns as the mutually available, human–machine "interface," one could compare and contrast them with the outer columns, as the respective interpretations of the user and the design. This comparison located precisely the points of confusion, as well as the points of true intersection or "shared understanding." Both are discussed at length in the next chapter.

7 Human–machine communication

> Interaction is always a *tentative* process, a process of
> continuously testing the conception one has of . . . the
> other.   (Turner 1962, p. 23, original emphasis)

In chapter 4, I outlined the view that the significance of actions, and
their intelligibility, resides neither in what is strictly observable
about behavior, nor in a prior mental state of the actor, but in a contingently constructed relationship between observable behavior,
embedding circumstances and intent. Rather than enumerating an
a priori system of normative rules for meaningful behavior, chapter
5 described resources for constructing shared understanding, collaboratively and *in situ*. Face-to-face interaction was presented as the
most fundamental and highly developed system for accomplishing
mutual intelligibility, exploiting a range of linguistic, demonstrative and inferential resources.

   Given this view of the basis for action's intelligibility, the situation of action can be defined as the full range of resources that the
actor has available to convey the significance of his or her own
actions, and to interpret the actions of others. Taking that preliminary definition of the situation as a point of departure, my interest
in this chapter is to consider "communication" between a person
and a machine in terms of the nature of their respective situations.
For purposes of the analysis, and without ascribing intent in any
way, I will assume that the machine is behaving on the basis of resources provided by "its" situation, the user in accord with the resources of hers. The aim of the analysis then is to view the
organization of human–machine communication, including its
troubles, in terms of constraints posed by asymmetries in the
respective situation resources of human and machine.

In the case considered here, we can assume that the situation of the user comprises preconceptions about the nature of the machine and the operations required to use it, combined with moment by moment interpretations of evidence found in and through the actual course of its use. The situation of the machine or expert help system, in contrast, is constituted by a plan for the use of the machine, written by the designer and implemented as the program that determines the machine's behavior, and sensors that register changes to the machine's state, including some changes produced by the user's actions. The design plan defines what constitutes intelligible action by the user insofar as the machine is concerned, and determines what stands as an appropriate machine response. The intersection of the situations of user and machine is the locus both for successful exploitation of mutually available resources, and for problems of understanding that arise out of the disparity of their respective situations.

7.1 Engineering an appropriate response

The practical problem with which the designer of an interactive machine must contend is how to ensure that the machine responds appropriately to the user's actions. As in human communication, an appropriate response implies an adequate interpretation of the prior action's significance. And as in human communication, the interpretation of any action's significance is only weakly determined by the action as such. Every action assumes not only the intent of the actor, but the interpretive work of the other in determining its significance.[1] That work, in turn, is available only through the other's response. The significance of any action and the adequacy of its interpretation is judged indirectly, by responses to actions taken, and by an interpretation's usefulness in understanding subsequent actions. It is just this highly contingent process that we call interaction.

[1] See Bruner (1986) for a recent discussion of this contingence of interpretation with respect both to text and to face-to-face interaction.

For purposes of analysis, we can begin by considering two alternative perspectives on face to face interaction, with commensurately different implications for the project of designing interactive machines. The first perspective ties successful interaction to each participant's success at anticipating the actions of the other, and recommends an interactive interface based on a preconceived model of the user that supports the prediction of actions, the specification of recognition criteria for the actions predicted, and the prescription of an appropriate response. The second view focuses on the ways in which interactional success comprises responses that are occasioned by, and responsive to, unanticipated actions of the other. This focus recommends an interactive interface that maximizes sensitivity to actions actually taken, by minimizing predetermined sequences of machine behavior. The former recommendation is constrained by limitations on the designer's ability to predict any user's actions, the latter by limitations on the system's access to and ability to make sense out of the actions that a particular user takes.

The design strategy in the expert help system is to try to provide the effect of an occasioned response, through the use of a predictive model. That is to say, the designer predicts that the user will have one of a set of possible goals, of the form "use the machine to accomplish outcome x." Given that statement of intent, the machine displays a set of instructions that prescribe the actions to be taken, at a level of generality designed to ensure their relevance to any user, whatever the details of her particular situation. Ideally, the instructions tell the user what aspects of her particular situation are relevant for the execution of this plan, and for the machine's operation. By finding or producing the objects and actions described, the user anchors the general instructions to her unique circumstances.

This chapter looks at some of the consequences of taking a statement of intent and an ascribed plan as grounds for the interpretation of situated action. To anticipate, that strategy involves an insensitivity to particular circumstances that is both the system's central resource, and its fundamental problem. I look first at the system's resources for construing the actions of the user; namely, *plans and states*. I then consider the problems posed for the designer by the user's principal resource, organized under the general rubric of *situated inquiries*, and by the user's ability to find the relevance of the system's response to those inquiries. Finally, I look at two classes of communicative breakdown, the *false alarm* and the *garden path*. Chapter 8 concludes with implications of the analysis for a general account of mutual intelligibility, and for the particular requirements on the design of artifacts that would interact with their users.

7.2 *The system's situation: plans and detectable states*

The resources of the expert help system include a program that controls its behavior, and sensors that register certain changes to its state effected by actions of the user. Initially, the user's response to a series of questions about her original documents and desired copies is taken as a statement of her intent, that statement in turn determining the selection by the machine of one from a set of possible plans (see display 0, p. 171). The plan is then presented to the user in the form of a step-wise set of procedural instructions. The designer assumes that the plan matches the user's intent, and that in following the procedural instructions, the user effectively is engaged in carrying out the plan.

The design premise is further that as the user takes the actions prescribed by the instructions, those actions will change the state of the machine in predictable ways. By taking those changes to the machine's state as traces of the user's actions, the designer can effectively specify how the user's actions are to be recognized by the system, and how the system is to respond. The instructions are grouped in a series of displays such that the last action prescribed by each display produces an effect that is detectable by the system, thereby initiating the process that produces the next display. The design assumption is that by detecting certain of the user's actions, the system can follow her course in the procedure and provide instructions as needed along the way.[2]

The strategy of tying certain machine states to the presentation of particular next instructions enables the appearance of machine responses occasioned by the user's actions. So, in this light, we can view the interaction between A and B in sequence 1 as the adept

Sequence 1. *A and B are proceeding from a display that established their goal as making two-sided copies of a bound document. (Two-sided copying requires an unbound document, so they must begin by making a master unbound copy of their document, using the "Bound Document Aid," or BDA.)*

THE USER		THE MACHINE	
Not available to the machine	Available to the machine	Available to the user	Design rationale
		DISPLAY 1	Selecting the procedure
		DISPLAY 2	Instructions for copying a bound document:
A: "To access the BDA, pull the latch labelled Bound Document Aid":: (Both A and B turn to the machine)			Accessing the Bound Document Aid.
(Points) Right there.			

[2] Because instructions were sometimes read by the users differently from the way they were actually written on the displays, the reader will find some inconsistencies between sequences and the displays to which they refer. The sequences comprise verbatim transcriptions of the users' talk. Double quotes indicate that the user is reading an instruction from the display.

The displays reproduce the visual presentation (both textual and illustrative) that the user finds on a video display terminal attached to the photocopier. This includes headings that identify the type of information offered (i.e. "Assumptions," "Overview," "Instructions"), the instructions themselves, and pictures of the copier and its parts. The boxed text at the bottom of each display (i.e. "Change Task Description," "Help," "Start") act as virtual "buttons" that, when selected by the user with the cursor provided, initiate an associated operation. "Change Task Description" returns the user to display 0, "Help" brings up a display that expands on the current instructions, "Start" begins the copying operation.

The system's situation: plans and detectable states

THE USERS		THE MACHINE	
Not available to the machine	Available to the machine	Available to the user	Design rationale

B: (Hands on latch)

A: "And lift up to the
left."
(Looks to B, who
struggles with the
latch)
"Lift up and to the
left."

B: (Still struggling)

A: Okay::

B: Pu::ll, and lift up
to the left.
(Looks at picture)
Oh, the whole thing
       [
A: Yea.
B: Lift up and to the
left.

| | **RAISES DOCUMENT HANDLER** | | |
| | | DISPLAY 3 | |

A: "Place your original
face down
(Passes journal to B)
on the glass, centered
over the registration
guide."
(Looks to machine)
Got that?
(pause)
Want me to read it
again?

      Instructions
for placing
document
and closing
document
cover.

B: Um:: I'm just trying
to figure out what
a registration guide is,
but I guess that's this,
um:

THE USERS		THE MACHINE	
Not available to the machine	Available to the machine	Available to the user	Design rationale
A: (Looking over her shoulder) Yea:			
B: centered over this line thingy here.			
A: Okay, let me read it again. "Place your original face down on the glass, centered over the registration guide, to position it for the copier lens." Okay?			
B: 'Kay.			
A: Okay. "Slide the document cover: left over your original until it latches."			

[Portion omitted in which users first mis-locate, then locate, the document cover.]

	CLOSES COVER		
		DISPLAY 4	Instructions to start printing
B: Okay, now, [			
A: All right:: "Press the Start button"			
	SELECTS START		

completion of what the design attempts. Specifically, A decomposes and re-presents the instructions provided by the system, such that they are fit more precisely to B's actions in carrying them out. A is able to do this because of her sensitivity to what B is doing, including B's troubles.

Below is the procedure from sequence 1, as represented in the program that controls the display of instructions to the user:

Step 1: Set Panel
   [DISPLAY 1]
Step 2: Tell User "You need to use the Bound Document Aid . . ."
   [DISPLAY 2]
Step 3: Tell User "Place your original face down . . . Slide the document cover left . . ."
   [DISPLAY 3]
Step 4: Make Ready.
Step 5: Tell User "Press Start." Requirements:
      Panel Set (If not, try Step 1)
      RDH raised (if not, try Step 2)
      Document cover closed (If not, try Step 3)
      Ready State (If not, try Step 4)
   [DISPLAY 4]
Step 6: Complete printing Step
   Requirements:
      Printing State (If not, try Step 5)

Rather than proceeding through the steps of the procedure consecutively, the system starts with the *last* step of the procedure, Step 6 in this case, and checks to see whether it is completed. A step is completed if a check of the machine's state confirms that the conditions represented by that step's requirements have been met. The requirements in this sense represent features of the system's situation (or, more accurately, of the system's own state) that are resources in determining an appropriate next instruction or action. When a requirement is found that is not met, a further set of specifications, tied to that requirement, sends the system back to an earlier step in the procedural sequence. The system then displays the instructions tied to that earlier step to the user, until another change in state begins the same process again. Each time the user takes an action that changes the machine's state, the system compares the resulting state with the end state, returns to the first unfinished step in the sequence, and presents the user with the instructions for that and any subsequent step.

Through this simple device of working backward through the procedure, the presentation of redundant instructions can be avoided. In sequence II, having discovered that their original document is larger than standard paper, A and B decide to re-do the job. They return to the job specification display to select the reduction feature, and then direct the machine to proceed.

Sequence II. *Again A and B are making two-sided copies of a bound document, this time with reduction. (The document is still on the copier glass, the document cover is closed.)*

THE USERS		THE MACHINE	
Not available to the machine	Available to the machine	Available to the user	Design rationale
		DISPLAY 1	Selecting the proceedure
B: It's supposed to— it'll tell "Start," in a minute.			
A: Oh. It will?			
B: Well it did: in the past. (pause) A little start: box will:			
		DISPLAY 4	Ready to print
B: There it goes.			
A: "Press the Start button"			
	SELECTS START		
		STARTS PRINTING	
Okay.			

On this occasion the system bypasses the instructions to raise the document handler, place the document on the glass, and close the document cover, all of which are irrelevant in that the actions they prescribe have already been taken. The system is able to act appropriately because a detectable machine state (the closed document cover) can be linked by the designer to an a priori assumption about the user's intent with respect to a next action (ready to press start). As a result, the system can be engineered to provide the appropriate next instruction *in spite of* the fact that it does not actually have access to the history of the user's actions, or even to the presence or absence now of a document on the glass. The result is that while B predicts the system's behavior – specifically, that it will provide them with a "Start button" – on her recollection of an occasion (sequence I) on which the system actually behaved somewhat differently, her prediction holds. That is, just because on this occasion a relevant feature of the user's situation, accessible to the system, causes the system to behave differently, it appears to behave in the "same," i.e. predictable way. In human interaction, this graceful accommodation to changing circumstance is precisely what is expected, and is therefore largely taken for granted. The success of the system's accommodation in this instance is evident in the accommodation's transparency to the users.

On other occasions, however, the mapping from a machine state to an a priori assumption about the user's intent, on which the success of sequence II rests, leads to trouble. I have said that given a statement of the user's goal (derived from answers to a series of questions about her originals and desired copies) the system initiates a plan, and then tracks the user's actions by mapping state changes to a step-wise procedure bound to that plan. In sequence III, A and B have completed the unbound master copy of their document, and have gone on to attempt to make their two-sided copies. They find that the page order in the copies is incorrect (a fault not available to the system, which has no access to the actual markings on the page), so they try again. As in sequence II, for them this is a second attempt to accomplish the same job, while for the machine it is just another instance of the procedure. On this occasion, however, that discrepancy turns out to matter.

Sequence III. *Again A and B are making two-sided copies from a bound document (this time having already completed their unbound master copy).*

THE USERS		THE MACHINE	
Not available to the machine	Available to the machine	Available to the user	Design rationale
B: Okay, and then it'll tell us,			
okay, and:: It's got to come up with the little start thing soon. (pause)		DISPLAY 1	Selecting the procedure
Okay, we've done all that. We've made our bound copies. (pause)		DISPLAY 2	Instructions for copying a bound document: Accessing the Bound Document Aid
A: It'll go on though, I think. Won't it?			
B: I think it's gonna continue on, after it realizes that we've done all that.			

In sequence II, the system's ignorance of the relation between this attempt to make copies and the last did not matter, just because a check of the current state of the machine caused the appropriate behavior. Or, more accurately, the "current state" of the interaction could be read as a local, technical matter independent of the embedding course of events. Here, however, a check of the machine's current state belies the users' intent. To appreciate what they are doing now requires that the relation between this attempt and the last *is* recognized, and the machine state does not capture that relation.

So while both users and system are, in some sense, doing the job again, there are two different senses of what, at this particular point, it means to do so. As far as the users are concerned, they are still trying to make two-sided copies of a bound document, so they leave their job description as such. For the machine, however, the appropriate description of their current goal, having made their master copy, is two-sided copying from an *unbound* document. The result is that what they in effect tell the machine they are doing is not what they intend to do, and what they intend to do is not available from the current state of the world as the machine is able to see it.

A and B find evidence of this trouble in an extended silence (sequence IV), which suggests that the system is not going to proceed (see also 7.4.2 below). What A and B discover here is that,

Sequence IV *(continued from III).*

THE USERS		THE MACHINE	
Not available to the machine	Available to the machine	Available to the user	Design rationale
		DISPLAY 2	Instructions for copying a bound document document
(8-sec. pause)			
A: Then again, maybe we need to change the task description.			
B: What do you think?			
	SELECTS "Change"		
		DISPLAY 0	User may want to change job description.
A: No.			
B: Okay, "Proceed."			
	SELECTS "Proceed"		

129

THE USERS		THE MACHINE	
Not available to the machine	Available to the machine	Available to the user	Design rationale
		DISPLAY 1	Making two-sided copies from a bound document
A: Maybe I should just lift it up and put it= [		DISPLAY 2	Accessing the Bound Document Aid
B: How do we skip this then?			
A: =down again. Maybe it'll think we're done.			
B: (laughs) Oh, Jean.			
A: There.	OPENS BDA		
		DISPLAY 3	Instructions for placing document
Okay, we've done what we're supposed to do.			
Now let's put this down. Let's see if that makes a difference. (Looks back to display)	CLOSES BDA		
		DISPLAY 2	Instructions for copying a bound document
(laughs) It did something.			
B: (inaudible) Good grief.			
A: Oh, it's still telling us we need to do a bound document.			

The system's situation: plans and detectable states

THE USERS		THE MACHINE	
Not available to the machine	Available to the machine	Available to the user	Design rationale
And we don't need to do the bound document because we've done that. You know, maybe we ought to go back to the beginning, and erase that thing about the bound document.			
B: Okay, that's a good idea.			
	SELECTS "Change"		
A: Then say, "Is it bound?" just put no.		DISPLAY 0	User may want to change job
B: Not anymore.			description
	SELECTS "No"		
A: And then everything else is constant, isn't it? It's on standard paper:: [			
B: so we'll proceed.			
	SELECTS "Proceed"		
A: So let's just proceed.			
			New job; two-sided from unbound document

from the system's "point of view," their intent is determined by their initial statement: that is, to make two-sided copies from a bound document. Statements of intent, however, are inevitably relative to larger purposes, and entail smaller ones, and while A and B's initial statement still accurately describes their global purpose, it belies their local one. Nor in this instance is their current situation (having failed successfully to produce the two-sided copies from their unbound master) reflected in the system's current state (ready to do two-sided copying from a bound original). Their current situation is available only through a history of which the system has no record, or through their reports and assertions about their situation, to which the system has no access. Their attempt to make their situation accessible to the system by exploiting its insensitivity to their actual circumstances and "faking" the required action fails, but the failure is a failure in performance not in principle. Specifically, if they had opened and closed the document *cover*, rather than only the Bound Document Aid, they would in fact have achieved the desired effect.

7.3 The user's resource: the situated inquiry

The premise of a self-explanatory machine is that users will discover its intended use through information found in and on the machine itself, with no need for further instruction. In physical design, for example, the designer anticipates certain questions such that, in the event, an answer is there ready at hand. So the user's question, "Where do I grab?" is answered by a handle fitted to the action of grabbing. In the traditional instruction manual, some further classes of inquiry are anticipated, and answers provided. The step-wise instruction set addresses the question "What do I do next?", and the diagram the question "Where?" In all cases, however, the questions anticipated and answered must be those that any user of the system might ask, and the occasion for both questions and answers is found by the user. It is this lack of "recipient design" in the written instruction manual that the expert help system is designed to redress.

For the novice engaged in a procedural task, the guiding inquiry is some form of the question "What next?" The question is an essentially indexical one, relying for its significance on the embedding situation. In the case at hand, the system effectively checks its own state to anticipate the user's question, and then presents the next outstanding requirement of the selected procedure in response. This design strategy assumes that the job specification represents the user's intent, that the intent so represented determines the appropriate plan, and that user and system are engaged in carrying out the procedure for that plan.

The design assumption, in other words, is that the situation of the question "What next?" is just the procedure, and that the question is a request for the next step. As long as that assumption holds, the presentation of a next instruction constitutes an appropriate response (see, for example, sequence i). The design assumption fails, however, in cases such as sequence v, where the question "What next?" is not a matter of *proceeding* with the current plan, but of its abandonment or *repair*. This sequence is discussed further

Sequence v. *C and D are making 5 two-sided copies of a bound document. (They are using the Bound Document Aid to make a single, unbound master copy of their original.)*

THE USERS		THE MACHINE	
Not available to the machine	Available to the machine	Available to the user	Design rationale
		DISPLAY 5	Instructions for copying a bound document: removing the document from the glass.
C: "Instructions. Slide the document cover to the right."			
D: (Noting output) Okay, it gave us one copy here.			
C: Okay, "Slide the document cover right to remove the original."			
D: We're supposed to have 5 copies and we only got one.			

THE USERS		THE MACHINE	
Not available to the machine	Available to the machine	Available to the user	Design rationale
C: (Looks to output) Oh. (Looks to display) We only got one?			
D: Yea.			
(long pause)			
C: *What do we do then?*			
(Long pause, both study display)			

below (see 7.5.1), but, for the moment, the observation is simply that the question "What do we do then?" is not, in this instance, a simple request for a "next" in the sense of a next step in the procedure, but rather is a request for a remedy to the current trouble. The situation of the inquiry (indicated anaphorically by the "then," viz. "given that we were supposed to have 5 copies and we only got one") is not the procedure itself, but the conflict between the apparent outcome of the procedure (a single copy), and their stated intent (five copies). That situation, while clearly described by D, is unavailable in the current state of the machine, which shows no evidence of their trouble. That is, the current state of the machine indicates just that a copy has been made, the design rationale being that they have copied the first page of an *unbound master copy* of their bound document, and are ready to go on to the second page.

As a consequence of the fact that the situation of their inquiry is not that which the design anticipates, and is not otherwise accessible to the system, the answer that the system offers – do the next step in this procedure – is inappropriate. Even in cases where the designer anticipates the need to remedy some trouble in the procedure rather than to go on to a next action, however, the context of a request for help may be problematic (sequence vi).

The selection of "Change task description," in the context of a

Sequence vi. *E and F and making two-sided copies of a bound document. (In response to the instruction to "close the document cover" (display 3), they have mistakenly closed the entire BDA instead, and as a consequence have returned to the previous instruction to open the BDA (display 2).)*

THE USERS		THE MACHINE	
Not available to the machine	Available to the machine	Available to the user	Design rationale
E: "Pull the latch labelled–" We did that. "Raise–" We did that. (Studying display) Okay. Okay.		DISPLAY 2	Instructions for copying a bound document
F: "Lift up on the latch," We did that.			
E: Now let's change::			
F: "Change task description?"			
E: Yes.			
F:	SELECTS "Change"		
"Describe the document to be copied–" Oh, we already did: No, we don't want to do that.		DISPLAY 0	User may want to change job specification
E: Maybe we have to do it to copy that. [i.e. the next page]			

THE USERS		THE MACHINE	
Not available to the machine	Available to the machine	Available to the user	Design rationale
F: (Looks around machine) (laugh) I don't know.			
E: Well::			
F: "Help" (laugh)			
	SELECTS "Help"		
		"Select the question you would like help with."	User needs clarification of display
E: I guess we still do have to= [			
F: We still ha–			
E: =answer this.			
F: Oh. okay, Alright.			
E: Okay.			
F: We sti– but we did all that, didn't we?			
E: Well, maybe not for this page.			

loop between display 2 and display 3, and their subsequent surprise at the re-appearance of display 0 in response, suggests that the intent of their action was not to return to the job specification, but to find a *next* instruction. The inherent ambiguity between any next instruction as either a continuation, or as the initiator of a repair, is discussed at length in 7.4. Our interest here is in the situation of the request for help that *follows* the return to display 0. Specifically, the selection of the "Help" option constitutes a question *about that return* to display 0, and the larger problem of the loop in which it is embedded. The design, however, takes the situation of the request to be a local one: that is, as having to do with interpreting the contents of display 0 itself.

Tied to the guiding inquiry "What next?" is a set of embedded questions about the prescribed actions – questions that look for clarification of the forms "How," "Where," or "To what," and "Why."[3] The system's responsiveness to requests for elaboration turns again on whether or not the designer successfully predicts the inquiry. In sequence VII C's question is actually interrupted by the change to display 2, which anticipates that very question. In this

Sequence VII. *C and D are making two-sided copies of a bound document.* *(They first must make a single, unbound master copy using the BDA.)*

THE USERS		THE MACHINE	
Not available to the machine	Available to the machine	Available to the user	Design rationale
		DISPLAY 1	Overview
C: "You need to use the Bound Document Aid to make an unbound copy of your original." Where is–			
Oh, here it is.		DISPLAY 2	Instructions for copying a bound document: picture of the BDA.

---

[3] From the standpoint of the actor concerned with a procedural next, the other two logically possible queries, viz. "By whom" and "When," are already answered by the embedding situation – though see sequences XVII and XXIII.

instance, it happens that the display change is timed to the mechanism that sets the machine's control panel, rather than being conditional on any action of the user's. Ironically, in part because on this occasion the system's behavior is determined *not* by the user's actions, but by the internal processing of the system, it appears that the system's behavior is occasioned by the user's question.

The fact that the question anticipated turns out to be the user's question in this instance marks the success of the design. In

Sequence VIII. *C and D are making two-sided copies from a bound document, using the BDA. (They have placed their document on the document glass.)*

THE USERS		THE MACHINE	
Not available to the machine	Available to the machine	Available to the user	Design rationale
C: Okay, wait a minute. "Slide the document cover left over your original until it latches." (Looks to machine)		DISPLAY 3	Copying a bound document: Closing the document cover
D: (Grasps BDA)			
C: The document cover– (leans over to look in BDA)			
D: Oh. (Pulls on document feeder belt, which gives a little) No, no, no. (indicating entire BDA) *This would be the document cover, isn't it?*			
C: *"To provide an eyeshield for the copier (inaudible)."*			

sequence VIII, however, the designer's prediction fails. In this case, the designer anticipates a question regarding the *motivation* for the action, while the user's problem is with the action's *object*. In sequence IX, the question *what is the object* is anticipated, while B's question actually concerns *how to do the action*. The answer to B's

Sequence IX. *A and B are making two-sided copies of an unbound document.*

THE USERS		THE MACHINE	
Not available to the machine	Available to the machine	Available to the user	Design rationale
A: "Place the copies:: on the top paper tray." [Portion omitted in which they locate the tray.] A: Okay. B: But, (Turning back to display) *How do you do that?* A: (Looking at diagram) *"The top paper tray is to the right of the output tray."* Place copies in the top paper tray," (Turning to tray) Oh, you just lift it up. (Does)		DISPLAY 11	Beginning second pass of two-sided copies

inquiry is found not in the instruction, which locates the object, but in the object itself. In sequence X, similarly, a problem in interpreting an instruction is solved through a picture of the object on which the action is to be performed.

Sequence x. *A and B are making two-sided copies of a bound document.*

THE USERS		THE MACHINE	
Not available to the machine	Available to the machine	Available to the user	Design rationale
A: "To access the BDA, pull the latch labelled Bound Document Aid"::		DISPLAY 2	Instructions for copying a bound document: Accessing the bound document aid.
(A and B turn to machine)			
(Points) Right there.			
B: (Hands on latch)			
A: "And lift up to the left." (Looks to B, who struggles with the latch) "Lift up and to the left."			
B: (Still struggling)			
A: Okay::			
B: Pu::ll, and lift up to the left. (Looks at picture) Oh, the whole thing= [			
A: Yea.			
B: =lift up and to the left.			
	Opens BDA		

When the object that B first takes to be implicated in the action description "lift up and to the left" resists her attempts to perform the action described, and the description suggests no other interpretation of the action, she finds in the picture a different object. That re-interpretation of the object, in its turn, revises the significance of the action description. In this way a conflict between the action on an object described by an instruction, and the action required by the object itself, can be a resource for identifying trouble in the interpretation of an instruction, and its resolution, as in sequence XI.

Sequence XI. *C and D have mistaken the entire BDA for the "document cover," and are caught in a loop between display 3 and display 2 (see also sequence VI).*

THE USERS		THE MACHINE	
Not available to the machine	Available to the machine	Available to the user	Design rationale
D: Okay. "Slide the document cover– left over your original, until it latches." (Turns to machine) You know it says "slide" – this (Finds document cover). Okay.		DISPLAY 3	Instructions for closing document cover
C: Ohh.			
D: (laughs) Ohh, isn't that hilarious? Okay. [			
C: Okay.			
	Closes cover		
		DISPLAY 4	
It was something else that was supposed to go over that.			

In general, the referential relationship between instructions and the actions and objects they describe is a reciprocal, rather than directional one. Burke (1982), for example, describes a pump assembly task in which to some extent all of the necessary information for assembling the pump is discoverable in requirements of the materials themselves, specifically the "fit and stay" bindings of one component of the pump to another. In spite of the constraints provided by the bindings, Burke noted a difference in confidence between those students who had additional linguistic instruction and those who did not, the former using the instructions, on the one hand, and the task actions and materials, on the other, as mutually informative, such that "both the instructions and the task actions are treated by the apprentice as problems to be solved. But each is used as a resource to solve the other as a problem" (p. 178). That is to say, while instructions answer questions about objects and actions, they also pose problems of interpretation that are solved in and through the objects and actions to which the instructions refer.

A nice example of this reciprocity of description and action described is shown in sequence XII. In this case, rather than the interpretation of the instruction "Pull the latch, etc." being *prerequisite* to the action's execution, the action, after the fact, clarifies what the instruction intends.

Sequence XII. *E and F are making two-sided copies of a bound document.*

THE USERS		THE MACHINE	
Not available to the machine	Available to the machine	Available to the user	Design rationale
F: "To access the BDA, pull the latch labelled Bound Document Aid." (Both turn to machine)		DISPLAY 2	Instructions for copying a bound document:
E: (Takes hold of latch)			Accessing the bound document aid.
F: Pull it down: just push it down.			

THE USERS		THE MACHINE	
Not available to the machine	Available to the machine	Available to the user	Design rationale
E: (Does, BDA starts to open)			
		DISPLAY 3	Placing the document on the glass
F: (startled) Oh, alright.			
	Opens BDA		
This is what you do.			
E: Is this what you do? Oh my gosh.			

Given the requests for clarification that are potential responses to any directive, one can easily predict that any one or more of them *might* occur, but not with any certainty *which*. The design of the expert help system attempts to deal with the problem exhaustively, and frequently succeeds. Questions of "How," "Where," and "Why" are answered by a diagram and supplementary description, provided with each next instruction. In all of these instances, however, the user brings the descriptions that the system provides to bear on the material circumstances of her situation, and brings those circumstances to bear on her interpretation of the descriptions. In other words, the user exploits the meaning of object and action descriptions to find their referents, and uses the objects and actions picked out as resources for finding the significance of the description. Through access to these resources the user not only asks, but also effectively answers her own situated inquiries.

7.4 *Conditional relevance of response*

We have seen how the responsiveness of the system is limited to those occasions where the users' actions effect some change in the machine's state, which ties the actions to the requirements of the underlying design plan. In principle, the design plan serves as the measure of what constitutes an adequate and appropriate action by the user: namely, one that satisfies the current procedural requirement. The requirements that the system imposes, in this procrustean sense, serve as prescriptions for successful use of the machine. The success assumes, however, that the user interprets the instructions and the system's responses in the way that the designer intended.

In the interest of conveying the intent of the design to the user, and in doing so interactively, the designer tacitly relies upon certain conventions of human conversation. Most generally, designer and user share the expectation that the relevance of each utterance is conditional on the last; that given an action by one party that calls for a response, for example, the other's next action will be a response. The expectation does not ensure that any next action in fact *will be* a response to the last, but it does mean that, wherever possible, the user will look for an interpretation of the next action that makes it so.

The user's expectation, in other words, is that each system response conveys, either implicitly or explicitly, an assessment of the last action she has taken and a recommendation for what to do next. More specifically, given some instruction to which the user responds with an action, the user has the following expectations with respect to the system's response:

(a) The system's response should be a new instruction, which stands as implicit confirmation of the adequacy of the user's previous action.
(b) If the system does not respond, the user's previous action is somehow incomplete.
(c) If the system's response is to repeat the instruction, the repetition implies that the user's previous action should be repeated (i.e. that the procedure is iterative) *or* that there is some trouble in the previous action that should be repaired.

7.4.1 *A new instruction confirms the previous action*

We have a general expectation, in carrying out a step-wise procedure, that completion of one action allows progress to a new instruction, and a next action. The correlate of the expectation that a completed action indicates readiness for a new instruction is the fact that the appearance of a new instruction is taken, at least initially, as confirmation of the previous action. In sequence XIII, B's evidence for the adequacy of A's action is simply the fact that it generates a response, which is assumed to be a next instruction. The apparent change to a new instruction confirms the preceding action in spite of the fact that the action description, "Slide the document cover," does not actually seem to fit the action taken.

Sequence XIII. *A and B are making two-sided copies of a bound document. (They first must make a single, unbound master copy using the BDA.)*

THE USERS		THE MACHINE	
Not available to the machine	Available to the machine	Available to the user	Design rationale
B: Okay. "Slide the document cover: left over your original, until it latches."		DISPLAY 3	Instructions for closing document cover
A: (Moves hand to BDA)			
B: (Turns to machine) "Slide the document cover," (Looks back to diagram) that's this [i.e. BDA]. Right?			
A: (Starts to close) We– it said left, though. (Looks to display)			
B: "To close the document cover, grasp the cover,			

THE USERS		THE MACHINE	
Not available to the machine	Available to the machine	Available to the user	Design rationale
A:	**CLOSES BOUND DOCUMENT AID**		
B: slide it firmly to the left."			
(You must) have done that.		DISPLAY 2	Instructions for opening Bound Document Aid

The action taken in fact is not closing the *document cover*, which is located inside the Bound Document Aid, but instead closing the Bound Document Aid itself. The assumption that display 2 must be a "next" to display 3, however, masks the fact that they are entering into a loop between those two displays (see also sequence VI).

7.4.2 No response indicates that the previous action is incomplete
In conversation, silences are more than just the absence of talk; they are generally owned by one party or another, and they invariably acquire significance (see chapter 5). The significance of silence lies in its relationship to the talk that it follows and, retrospectively, the talk that it can be seen to precede. In particular, the convention that certain utterance types (questions and answers being the canonical example) sequentially implicate the appropriate next utterance produces "noticeable absences" when the next is not forthcoming. An extended silence following a question, for example, will be seen as a non-response. In the case of the expert help system, there is no response until the user completes the action prescribed by the final instruction of a given display. This design constraint, combined with the user's expectation from human interaction regarding sequential implicature and silence, means that the unresponsive-

ness of the system carries information. Specifically, when an action that is intended to satisfy a final instruction fails to elicit a response, the user takes the unresponsiveness as evidence for trouble in her performance of the action. In sequence XIV, for example, what C and D initially see as a pause comes to be seen, in virtue of its length, as a non-response. The non-response, in turn, carries information with respect to their last action. Specifically, the non-response indicates that this is still, in effect, their turn: that the last action was not, somehow, the action prescribed by this instruction. The evidence that the non-response provides – that there is some problem in the action taken – initiates a re-inspection of the instruction, a re-identification of the instruction's object, and the action's repair.

Sequence XIV. *C and D are making two-sided copies using the "Recirculating Document Handler" or RDH.*

THE USERS		THE MACHINE	
Not available to the machine	Available to the machine	Available to the user	Design rationale
		DISPLAY 10 [see p. 176]	Copies complete
C: Okay, "Remove the copies from the output tray." (Takes documents from document handler) Okay. Now:			
(15-second pause)			
(Turns to output) Oh, (Looks back to display)			
D: The output tray:			
C: This is the output tray.			
D: (Points to picture) That's the output tray, okay.			

7.4.3 Repetition is ambiguous between iteration and repair

There are two conditions on which the system may repeat a prior instruction:

(a) The action taken in response to the instruction should be repeated (the common case, for example, in a procedure that is *iterative*);

(b) The action taken in response to the instruction *is in error* in just such a way as to return the system to a state prior to the instruction: in effect, to undo a previous action. This produces a *loop*.

In human interaction, (b) does not occur. On the other hand, in human interaction repetition is used in a way that does not occur between user and machine, namely to indicate that:

(c) The action taken in response to the instruction in some way fails to satisfy the intent of the instruction, and needs to be remedied.

Consistent with the observation that users import expectations from human interaction to construe the system's responses, users fail to recognize the occurrence of (b), and instead read all cases of repetition as either (a) or as (c).

Repetition as iteration. In procedural instructions, there are occasions, illustrated in sequence xv, on which the repeat of an instruction is to be taken at face value, as an explicit directive to do the previous action again.

Purposeful action is characterized by the fact that its projected outcome is a resource for assessing the action's course. Where the procedure is a composite one, this function is complicated, however. For one thing, success at a composite procedure depends on reliable ways of discriminating between the procedure's outcome and its intermediate states. Particularly for the novice, the expectation that an embedded procedure (in this case, making the

Sequence xv. *A and B are making two-sided copies of a bound document.*
(They have copied the first page of the document, using the BDA.)

THE USERS		THE MACHINE	
Not available to the machine	Available to the machine	Available to the user	Design rationale
B: "If more pages are to be copied, then place the next page face down on the glass."		DISPLAY 6	Iterative procedure for using the BDA
A: Just keep it up until we're finished with the, with the, uh:			
B: Oh, well how do you– she was– she said on both sides, right?			
A: Well that's after we finish getting this (indicating document). We're just getting the originals to stick up here [i.e. RDH].			
B: Oh, you're right, you're right.			

unbound master copy of the document) will produce the *finished* product leads to confusion like that of B in sequence xv, and to more complex misunderstandings, as shown in sequence xvi.

Coming to what they take to be the end of the iterative procedure described in display 6, C and D hypothesize that their part in the procedure is finished, that the next turn is the system's. That hypothesis is challenged by the system's inaction (a silence of eleven seconds), which suggests some incompleteness in their own action, and something further for them to do. Their problem, then, is to

Sequence xvi. *C and D are making 5 two-sided copies of a bound document. (They have completed the* master *copy using the BDA. Unaware of the composite structure of the procedure, and seeking to explain the fact that this procedure has produced only one copy, they have adopted the hypothesis that the remaining four copies are produced automatically, by the machine, and they are waiting for them to appear.)*

THE USERS		THE MACHINE	
Not available to the machine	Available to the machine	Avaliable to the user	Design rationale
		DISPLAY 6	Iterative procedure for using the BDA: when RDH is lowered,
D: "Place the next page face down on the glass. Slide the document cover (inaudible). Lower the RDH until it latches." (pause) Okay.			
(11-second pause)			user is ready to
So we start over for five? It doesn't do it (inaudible)?			go on to make multiple
C: I guess we just have to do it five times, and then it'll: (pause) Do what it says, I guess.			copies

find a "next": that is, some action prescribed by the instructions that is outstanding.[4] Given that problem, and its situation in the inherently ambiguous context of a procedure that is both recursive and composite (copying each page once until the end of the document, in order that the document can be copied five times), one possible solution is to see the persistence of this instruction as a repeat rather than a non-response, and therefore as a directive to do the procedure again.

[4] The outstanding instruction, in fact, is "Lower the RDH until it latches." For the designer, that is the precondition for continuing on to the second pass of the procedure. For the users, however, under the assumption that the procedure is effectively completed, that could only be a sort of coda (like putting away the bowls once one has baked a cake), with no direct consequence for the outcome.

Conditional relevance of response

In another case, sequence XVII, the option "Change task description," intended by the designer to enable a repair, but noticed in the context of the search for a next turn, suggests iteration where the designer did not intend it. If E and F's objective in selecting

Sequence XVII. *E and F are in a loop between display 3 and display 2*

THE USERS		THE MACHINE	
Not available to the machine	Available to the machine	Available to the user	Design rationale
E: "Pull the latch labelled–" We did that. "Raise–" We did that. (Studying display) Okay. Okay.		DISPLAY 2	Instructions for copying a bound document: Raising the document handler.
F: "Lift up on the latch," We did that.			
E: Now let's change::			
F: "Change task description?"			
E: Yes.			
F:	SELECTS "Change"		
"Describe the document to be copied–" Oh, we already did: No, we don't want to do that.		DISPLAY 0	User may want to change job specification
E: Maybe we have to do it to copy that [i.e. the next page].			
F: (Looks around machine) (laugh) I don't know.			

"Change task description" is to find a next action, one way that they can make the system's response a relevant one is to interpret the return to display o iteratively, as telling them to specify their job again. The possibility, if not plausibility, of that interpretation arises from the fact that the difference between going "backward" to something already done in a procedure, and going "forward" to repeat the action, is inherently problematical. The difference does not lie in any features of the instruction or action itself, but just in whether the instruction's re-appearance at a given time is read as a misunderstanding, or as intended by the design. (See sequence VI above for the development of the problem.)

Finally, the novice user may *expect* iteration in what is by design a one-pass procedure. C's action in sequence XVIII of removing the first page of the document and replacing it with a second assumes that this procedure is iterative, viz. copy each page one at a time, until finished. While taken as a next, however, her action restores a state that from the system's "point of view" appears identical to the state *before* the action was taken – a document in the document handler – thereby cancelling the action's effect. For C, logically, the *last* page has been removed from the document handler, and putting the *next* page in is pre-requisite to going on; for the system there is just *a* document in the document handler, and its *removal* is required to go on.

Seen as an instruction to undo their last action, the instruction to "remove the original" would stand as evidence of trouble. But by paraphrasing "remove" as "move the first page to make a place for the second," C makes this response relevant by turning it into a next, iterative instruction, and therefore a confirmation of her last action. (For discussion of this sequence as a "garden path," see section 7.5 below.)

Repetition as repair. The inclination to see each next instruction as a new instruction means that a repetition might not initially even be recognized as such. Recall that this was the case in sequence XIII. In fact, this is another instance of the loop described for sequence VI.

Sequence xviii. *C and D are making 4 one-sided copies of an unbound document, using the RDH.*

THE USERS		THE MACHINE	
Not available to the machine	Available to the machine	Available to the user	Design rationale
C: Okay, and face up, Right? First page?		DISPLAY 7	Instructions for copying an unbound document: Place all originals in RDH.
	DOCUMENT PLACED IN DOCUMENT HANDLER		
"Press the Start button." Where's the Start button? (Looks around machine, then to display)		DISPLAY 8	Ready to print
D: (Points to display) Start? Right there it is.			
C: There. (laughs)			
D: Okay.			
C:	SELECTS START		
		STARTS	Document is being copied
		DELIVERS COPIES	Job complete
Ta:: Oh, it comes right back out.			
		DISPLAY 9	Removing originals
	REMOVES DOCUMENT		

THE USERS		THE MACHINE	
Not available to the machine	Available to the machine	Available to the user	Design rationale
So it made four of the first? (Looks at display) Okay.			
		DISPLAY 10	Removing copies from the output tray.
(Holding second page over the document handler, looks to display)			
Does it say to put it in yet?			
D: (inaudible) "Remove the copies from the output tray."			
C: (inaudible) number two. (Puts second page into document handler)			
	DOCUMENT PLACED IN DOCUMENT HANDLER		
		DISPLAY 9	Removing originals
"Remove the original–" Okay, I've re- I've moved the original. And put in the second copy.			

Specifically, in sequence XIII mislocation of the object referred to as the "document cover" leads B to close the entire Bound Document Aid, an action that returns the system to its initial state and causes it to re-display the first instruction, namely, to open the BDA.[5] The

---

[5] Fortuitously, the action that the BDA suggests, just because it returns the machine to a previous state, is the only action other than that which the design intends to which the system would respond at all at this point.

design rationale that produces this system response is simple: (i) the user must use the BDA to copy bound documents; (ii) in order to use the BDA, it must be opened; (iii) if the BDA is closed, the user should be presented with instructions for opening it. However, rather than taking the return to the previous instruction as evidence for some problem in their last action, A and B see it as a next instruction, and as confirmation.

The inclination to mistake a return to a previous instruction for a next can be appreciated by considering the anomalous character of this particular problem in terms of any parallels in human interaction. While repetition of the first part of an adjacency pair is justified in cases where there is no response, when a response does occur it terminates the sequence and provides for the relevance of a next. Insofar as the user believes her action constitutes a response to the current instruction, then, she has every reason to view the system's next turn as a next instruction. The closest situation that one finds in human interaction to the loop in human–machine communication occurs when a response to a sequentially implicative utterance – the answer to a summons, for example – is not recognized as such:

> As noted, upon the completion of the SA [summons–answer] sequence, the original summoner cannot summon again. The operation of this terminating rule, however, depends upon the clear recognition that an A has occurred. This recognition normally is untroubled. However, trouble sometimes occurs by virtue of the fact that some lexical items, e.g., "Hello," may be used both as summonses and as answers. Under some circumstances it may be impossible to tell whether such a term has been used as summons or as answer. Thus, for example, when acoustic difficulties arise in a telephone conversation, both parties may attempt to confirm their mutual availability to one another. Each one may them employ the term "Hello?" as a summons to the

other. For each of them, however, it may be unclear whether what he hears in the earpiece is an answer to his check, or the other's summons for him to answer. One may, under such circumstances, hear a conversation in which a sequence of some length is constituted by nothing but alternatively and simultaneously offered "hellos." Such "verbal dodging" is typically resolved by the use, by one party, of an item on which a second is conditionally relevant, where that second is unambiguously a second part of a two-part sequence. Most typically this is a question, and the question "Can you hear me?" or one of its common lexical variants, regularly occurs. (Schegloff 1972, p. 366)

Recognized as such, a return to a previous instruction that cannot be construed as iterative is evidence for trouble. In sequence XIX is another instance of the same misunderstanding that we saw in sequence XIII.

In human interaction, when the response to an action is either incoherent or inappropriate, the producer of the original action has recourse to two possible interpretations. She can treat the troublesome response as the product of an error on the listener's part (not hearing or mishearing, not understanding or misunderstanding), or as intended. If the troublesome response is seen as the product of some failure of hearing or understanding, the repair may be just to repeat the original action (see Coulter 1979, p. 30). Unless the trouble is one of hearing, however, we rarely repeat a directive verbatim if there appears to be some problem of understanding the first time around. Instead, we try some reformulation, or elaboration. If one formulation fails to convey our intended meaning, we try another. Frequently, it is not simply that we try an alternative formulation of what we intended before, but that what we intend is conditional on the others' response. In that sense, our own intentions are clarified for us by the response of the other.

In every case, to the extent that we are heard to be repeating ourselves, the repeat is heard as an attempt to correct some problem in

Sequence xix. *E and F are making two-sided copies of a bound document.*
(They first must make a single, unbound master copy using the BDA.)

THE USERS		THE MACHINE	
Not available to the machine	Available to the machine	Available to the user	Design rationale
		DISPLAY 3	
F: "Slide the document cover over your original until it latches." E: (Hand on BDA) F: Just push it down. E:	CLOSES BDA		
		DISPLAY 2	
Okay, here we go. (turns to display) "Pull the latch la–" Oh, we already did that.			
(pause. They study display)			
E: Okay.			
F: Okay.			
(7-second pause)			
Now what do we do?			

understanding the first time around (see Jordan and Fuller 1974).
Seen in this light, as a repair-initiator, repetition initiates a review
of the repeated instruction. In sequence xx, a review of the instruction confirms that the actions it prescribes have been done. The two
alternative responses to the repeat, in that case, are either to assert
that the action is complete, or to do it again. In face-to-face interaction these alternatives appear to be ordered; that is, we first assert
that we have heard a prior utterance and responded to it and then,
if the assertion does not suffice, we provide a demonstration. Realizing that in communication with the machine assertions never

suffice, that the system has access only to demonstrations or actions, is part of acquiring proficiency in its use.

Sequence xx *(continued from XIX).*

THE USERS		THE MACHINE	
Not available to the machine	Available to the machine	Available to the user	Design rationale
		DISPLAY 2	

E: "Pull the latch labelled–"
We did that.
"Raise–"
We did that.
(Studying display)
Okay. Okay.

F: "Lift up on the latch,"
We did that.

Actually re-doing an action frequently uncovers problems of understanding, not just because the same terrain is considered again, but because, considered again, the terrain is seen differently, as in sequence xxi. On the other hand, when a review fails to reveal any

Sequence xxi. *Another case of the loop between display 2 and display 3.*

THE USERS		THE MACHINE	
Not available to the machine	Available to the machine	Available to the user	Design rationale
		DISPLAY 2	

B: "Pull the latch labelled bound," "Raise the RDH."
"To access the BDA, pull the latch labelled Bound Document Aid,"
Okay, (Gesture to latch, then back to display) we did.

A: Yea.

158

THE USERS		THE MACHINE	
Not available to the machine	Available to the machine	Available to the user	Design rationale

B: "And lift up to the left,"
    do it again.

A:

                                       OPENS TO
                                         BDA

                                                                DISPLAY 3

   There. (To display)
   I'm lifting
   up to the left.

B: Okay.
   "Place your original
   face down on the glass,
   centered over the
   registration=
   [
A: "guide," Okay.
   [

B: =guide."

A: Did that.

B: "Slide the document co–"

A: "cover left over=
   [

B: Wait a minute.

A: =your originals,"
   Well:

B: Here's the document glass,
   (Indicating BDA)
   is that what they mean?

A: (Looking at BDA)
   Document cover.

THE USERS		THE MACHINE	
Not available to the machine	Available to the machine	Available to the user	Design rationale
B: "To close the document cover, grasp the cover and slide it firmly to the left."			
A: (Finding it) Oh, here's the document cover!			
	CLOSES DOCUMENT COVER		
B: Oh, Jean, good girl!			
A: There's the document–			
		DISPLAY 4	
(Both turn back to display)			
Okay, now: [			
B: All right: "Press: the Start button." Jean, you're doin' great.			
	SELECTS "Start"		
(Both look to BDA)		MACHINE STARTS	
A: Oh, I see, [			
B: Alright.			
A: We don't have to close this big thing.			
B: No, we were– we were lookin' at the wrong thing. We were closing the bound document aid, instead of the:			
A: instead of the document cover.			

new actions, a reasonable inference is that the next action must be the other's. In sequence XXII, C's review indicates that the actions prescribed by the instructions have all been completed; the sense of her "ready" here is as in "ready to go." There appears to be nothing further for them to do. Since the logical next is for the machine to

Sequence XXII. *Again, another case of the loop between display 2 and display 3.*

THE USERS		THE MACHINE	
Not available to the machine	Available to the machine	Available to the user	Design rationale
		DISPLAY 2	
C: (inaudible, rereads instructions) Okay, are we ready? "Pull the latch labelled bound– to release." and then you release:: the, uh, RDH (inaudible.) Okay, are we ready? (pause) Oh, it's supposed to do it by itself. (pause)			

copy the document, C concludes that it must do so without further action on their part. Concluding that it is the system's turn offers an alternative to the original interpretation of the repeat as an indication that their action is somehow incomplete. If the system is in fact responding to their last action, that both confirms the action's adequacy, and accounts for the system's failure to provide a next instruction.

The length of time that passes with no apparent activity, however, casts doubt on that conclusion, as the system's silence takes on the character of a non-response. If the system is not responding, there must be some further action for them to take. In sequence XXIII, they again attempt to read the repetition as a directive to repair some problem in the action as it was done the first time through. C's "why" here is a locally situated one; that is, she is not

Sequence XXIII *(continued from XXII).*

THE USERS		THE MACHINE	
Not available to the machine	Available to the machine	Available to the user	Design rationale
		DISPLAY 2	
C: "Pull the latch labelled bound copy aid to release the– RDH"			
D: (Points) This is the RDH. This [i.e. the latch] is the release.			
C: *But why does it want it to release it?* (To display) "Release (inaudible) to enable placement of the bound document on the glass," so we don't have that on the glass like it's supposed to be.			

asking in general about the rationale for this instruction, but in particular about its intent now, given their history and present circumstances. While the answer provided is intended to justify the instruction on *any* occasion, she attributes to it a significance particular to *this* occasion. Because their inquiry is situated in their particular circumstances, the answer is taken as an answer to that situated inquiry. Specifically, C reads the "to enable" clause as relevant to the directive that they release the RDH again, to allow a repair of some fault in the document's placement. This attributes to the system substantially greater sensitivity than it has: namely, the ability to tell how the document is sitting on the glass, and to notice that it is faulted in some way. Under this interpretation of the design, the directive to re-place the document would be conveyed by re-presenting this instruction to the user until the document is placed correctly. This interpretation not only accounts for the loop in which they've found themselves, but also suggests the way out of it.

7.5 *Communicative breakdowns*

Users of the expert help system encounter two forms of communicative breakdown: the *false alarm* and the *garden path*. In the first case, a misconception on the user's part leads her to find evidence of an error in her actions where none exists; in the second, a misconception on the user's part produces an error in her action with respect to the prescribed procedure, the presence of which is masked. In neither case is the breakdown available as such to the system.

7.5.1 *The false alarm*
I noted earlier that purposeful action is characterized by the fact that projected outcomes of action are a resource for producing the action's course. In particular, the effects of actions taken are compared against expected outcomes, in order to judge the action's adequacy. Expectations with respect to the effect of actions taken often are not articulated, but are discovered only in the breach. In sequence xxiv the machine offers the users two competing pieces of evidence regarding the adequacy of their last action. The display offers a next instruction, which makes sense as a confirmation of their previous action. The output, however, indicates that the action has failed, in which case the next instruction is irrelevant. From the system's "point of view," nonetheless, there is no problem. And because the system detects no problem here, it offers no

163

Sequence XXIV. *C and D are making two-sided copies of a bound document. (They have copied the first page.)*

THE USERS		THE MACHINE	
Not available to the machine	Available to the machine	Available to the user	Design rationale
		DISPLAY 5	Copying a bound document: Opening the document cover
C: "Instructions. Slide the document cover to the right."			
D: (Noting output) Okay, it gave us one copy here.			
C: Okay, "Slide the document cover right to remove the original."			
D: We're supposed to have 5 copies and we only got one.			
C: (Looks to output) Oh. (Looks to display) We only got one?			
D: Yea. (long pause)			
C: What do we do then?			
(long pause, Both study display)			

prescription for a remedy. The result is an interactional impasse, where the question "What do we do then?" finds no answer. Or rather, the answer that the system provides makes sense only if what the users intend to do is to continue making a single copy from a bound document.[6]

[6] The problem here is one of intermediate states vs. outcomes. The procedure for two-sided copying requires use of the Recirculating Document Handler, but use of that mechanism requires an unbound original. As a consequence of that mechanism constraint, the first pass of the procedure for copying a bound document is directed at producing one, unbound, master copy of the document. This requires a procedure of copying each page, using the Bound Document Aid, until there is one

While from the point of view of the design that is precisely what they want to do, that intent is not a feature of *their* situation. Their situation, meanwhile – that they intended to produce five copies of the document, and have produced only one – is unavailable to the system. The consequence is that the users ascribe a (spurious) misunderstanding of their intent to the machine, while the machine fails to detect the (genuine) misunderstanding on their part with respect to the structure of the procedure. The result is their effort to repair a line of action that is in no way faulty.

7.5.2 *Garden path*

To the extent that different assumptions of users and designers produce evidence of misunderstanding, there is at least some hope that the trouble might be located and resolved. In 7.4 we looked at two events taken by users as evidence of trouble: namely, the nonresponse and the repeat. As in sequence xxiv, false expectations with respect to an action's effect may lead the user to find evidence for trouble in her performance where, in design terms, none exists. Because in such cases the problem lies in the user's expectations rather than her actions, and because the evidence for her expectations that the user provides is unavailable to the machine, the problem itself is unavailable to the machine.

While the user is uncertain of her action in such cases, the action she takes is in fact the action that the design prescribes. Deeper problems arise when the user takes an action other than that prescribed by the design, but one that satisfies the procedural requirement. As a result of the ambiguity of the action's effect, the incorrect action is actually "mistaken" by the system for some other, correct action, from which it is indistinguishable by the system's sensors. As in xxiv, the problem in such cases is inaccess-

---

complete set to be put into the RDH. While an overview of the procedure was presented in display 1, designed to correct the assumption that this first pass would produce the desired outcome directly, the overview evidently did not do so. D's statement of the problem demonstrates their continuing confusion, but the fact that the confusion is unavailable to the system precludes what would be a second chance for the misconception's repair.

ible to the system. But whereas in xxiv the misconception leads the user to find evidence of trouble where, by design, none exists, in these other cases trouble is masked by the fact that the user sees the action as non-problematic, and by the fact that because the action appears non-problematic to the system as well, the system's response appears to the user to confirm the action.

Take the example in sequence xviii (above, p. 153). From the system's "point of view," this sequence produces no evidence of trouble. Display 7 instructs the users to place their documents in the Recirculating Document Handler and the system's sensors "see" them do so; display 8 instructs them to press Start; they do, and the machine produces four copies of their document.

To a human observer with any knowledge of this machine, however, C's question "So it made four of the first?" indicates a misunderstanding. Specifically, her question conveys the information that this in fact is not a single-page document, but the first page of several. And in contrast to other machines that require the placement of pages on the glass one at a time, copying an unbound document of multiple pages with this machine requires loading the pages all at once. The problem here is not simply a failure of anticipation on the designer's part. On the contrary, in anticipation of this very situation, the instruction for loading documents explicitly states that *all* of the pages should be placed in the document handler. There is no evidence, however, that the instruction is consulted by these users.

One basic premise of instructions is that they explicate a problem of action: if there is no problem, there is logically no need for instruction. We can infer from the users' failure to consult the instructions at this point that they have a preconception about what to do, based on past experience. Such preconceptions probably account in large part for the common complaint from designers that people "ignore" instructions; they ignore them because they believe that they already know how to proceed. But given the fact of the users' misconception, the further problem arises when the faulted action goes by unnoticed at the point where it occurs. It does so because what is available to the system is only the action's effect, and that effect satisfies the requirements for the next instruction. As an assertion in the form of a question, C's statement not only formulates her view of the system's last operation, but requests confirmation of that formulation. Interactionally, her statement provides an occasion for the discovery of the misunderstanding. She even looks to the display for a response. The information provided there is efficient enough, however – it simply says, "The copies have been made" – to support her assertion, rather than challenge it. As a consequence, the misunderstanding displayed in C's question is unavailable to the system, while the efficiency of the system's response masks the trouble for the user.

C's action of placing the document in the document handler appears, in other words, to be a perfectly adequate response to display 7. The system treats the action as satisfying the directive to place all of the documents in the document handler (where "all" in this case comprises one), and therefore provides a next instruction, while C and D take the appearance of the next instruction as confirmation that their last action, placing *the first page* of their document in the document feeder, satisfied the design intent. The start-up of the machine, with no complaint about their prior action, reflects the fact that the directive to "Start" has two different, but compatible interpretations. For the users, the significance of the directive is "make 4 copies of page 1," while for the system it is just "make 4 copies of the document in the document handler." There is nothing in either display 9 or display 10 to indicate the discrepancy. Each is efficient enough to be read under either interpretation.

So at the point where the machine starts to print, C is making four copies of page 1 of her document, while the machine is just making four copies of the document in the document handler. This seems, on the face of it, a minor discrepancy. If the machine copies the document, why should it matter that it fails to appreciate more finely the document's status as one in a set of three?

The problem lies in the consequences of this continuing misunderstanding for the next exchange. The strength of C's conception of what is going on (repeating the procedure for each page) provides her with a logical next action (loading her second page into the document handler) in advance of any instruction. The instruction is looked to for confirmation of her action, rather than for direction. Her certainty is evident in the terms of the question: "Does it say to put it in yet?" The deictic pronoun "it" with respect to the system as "next speaker," and to the second page as the object of the instruction, the "in" with respect to the location of the action, and the "yet" with respect to the time of the action, all imply a shared situation that would make the interpretation of those indexical terms non-problematic. For C, that the instruction will appear and what it will say is not in question – only when. While C is going on to the next run of the procedure, however, the system is still engaged in the completion of the last. What remains is the *removal* of originals and copies from their respective trays.

The "misunderstanding" between users and system at this point turns on just what the document in the document handler is, and how it got there. For C, a first page has been replaced by a second, a necessary step for the next pass of what she takes to be an iterative procedure. For the system, there just is *a* document in the document handler, and its removal is required for the procedure's completion. The result is an impasse wherein both user and system are "waiting for each other," on the assumption that their own turn is complete, that their next action waits on an action by the other.

The instruction to "Place all of your originals in the RDH" must be designed for any user who might come along, on any occasion. The designer assumes that on some actual occasion the instruction, in particular the relative quantifier "all," will be anchored by the particular user to a particular document with a definite number of pages. Under the assumption that the user will do that anchoring, the system just takes the evidence that *something* has been put into the RDH as an appropriate response, and takes whatever is put there as satisfying the description. On the one hand, this means that the system can provide the relevant instruction in spite of the fact that it does not have access to the particular identities of this user, or this document. On the other hand, the system's insensitivity to particulars of this user's situation is the limiting factor on its ability to assess the significance of her actions.

7.6 Summary

This analysis has tied the particular problem of designing a machine that responds appropriately to the actions of a user, to the general problem of deciding the significance of purposeful action. The ascriptions of intent that make purposeful action intelligible, and define a relevant response, are the result of inferences based on linguistic, demonstrative, and circumstantial evidence. I have argued that one way to characterize machines is by the severe constraints on their access to the evidential resources on which human communication of intent routinely relies. In the particular case considered here, the designer of the expert help system attempts to circumvent those constraints through prediction of the user's actions, and detection of the effects of actions taken. When the actual course of action that the user constructs proceeds in the way that the design anticipates, effects of the user's actions can be mapped to the projected plan, and the system can be engineered to provide an appropriate response.

The new user of a system, however, is engaged in ongoing, situated inquiries regarding an appropriate next action. While the instructions of the expert help system are designed in anticipation of the user's inquiries, problems arise from the user's ability to move easily between a simple request for a next action, "meta" inquiries about the appropriateness of the procedure itself, and embedded requests for clarification of the actions described within a procedure. In reading the machine's response to her situated inquiries and taking the actions prescribed, the user imports certain expectations from human communication: specifically, that a new instruction in response to an action effectively confirms the adequacy of that action, while a non-response is evidence that the action is incomplete. In the case of repeated instructions, an ambi-

guity arises between interpreting the repetition as a straightfor-
ward directive to repeat the action, or as a directive for its repair. A
further problem arises when the action that the user takes in
response to an instruction is in error in just such a way as to return
the system to a state prior to that instruction. Because this trouble
does not arise in human interaction, new users initially fail to recognize the occurrence of such a loop.

Due to the constraints on the machine's access to the situation of
the user's inquiry, breaches in understanding that for face-to-face
interaction would be trivial in terms of detection and repair become
"fatal" for human–machine communication (see Jordan and Fuller
1974). In particular, misconceptions with regard to the structure of
the procedure lead users to take intermediate states of the procedure as faulted outcomes. Because the intermediate state is non-
problematic from the system's point of view, the system offers no
remedy. The result is an interactional impasse, with the user finding evidence of trouble in her actions where none in fact exists. In
the case of the garden path, in contrast, the user takes an action that
is in some way faulted, which nonetheless satisfies the requirements of the design under a different but compatible interpretation. As a result, the faulty action goes by unnoticed at the point
where it occurs. At the point where the trouble is discovered by the
user, its source is difficult or impossible to reconstruct.

Describe the document to be copied:

Is it a bound document? [Yes] [No]

Copy both sides of each sheet? [Yes] [No]

Is it on standard size (8.5″ × 11″) paper? [Yes] [No]

Is it on standard thickness paper? [Yes] [No]

Quality of original: [darker than normal] [normal] [lighter than normal]

About how many images are to be copied?

	1	
1	2	3
4	5	6
7	8	9
	0	Clear

Describe the desired copies:

Number of copies:

	1	
1	2	3
4	5	6
7	8	9
	0	Clear

Use standard paper? [Yes] [No]

Staple each copy? [Yes] [No]

Put images on both sides? [Yes] [No]

Reduce size of images? [No] [35% smaller] [20% smaller] [2% smaller]

[PROCEED]   [HELP]

Display 0   Job specification: The user describes her original document
and the desired copies by selecting one of the options following each
question. The number of images to be copied and number of copies
desired are specified by selecting numbers on the associated "keypad."
"Proceed" and "Help" act as virtual "buttons"; when selected,
"Proceed" invokes the next display in the series (i.e. the first of a set of
procedural instructions), while "Help" provides some explanation of
each of the questions in display 0 itself.

OVERVIEW:

You need to use the
Bound Document Aid (BDA)
to make an unbound
copy of your original.
That copy can then be
put into the Recirculating
Document Handler (RDH)
to make your collated
two-sided copies.

INSTRUCTION:

Please wait.

THE COPIER

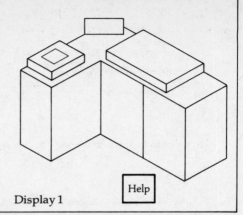

Change Task Description	

Display 1

Help

OVERVIEW:

You need to use the
Bound Document Aid (BDA)
to make an unbound copy
of your original.
That copy can then be
put into the Recirculating
Document Handler (RDH)
to make your collated
two-sided copies.

INSTRUCTION:

Pull the latch labelled
Bound Document Aid.
(to release the RDH).

Raise the RDH
(to enable placement
of the bound document
on the glass).

How to access the BDA:

To access the BDA,
pull the latch labelled
Bound Document Aid,

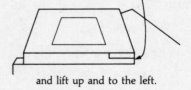

and lift up and to the left.

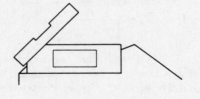

Change Task Description	

Display 2

Help

172

INSTRUCTION:

Place your original
face down on the glass,
centered over the
registration guide
(to position it for the copier lens).

Slide the document cover
left over your original
until it latches
(to provide an eye shield
from the copier lights).

How to close the document cover:

To close the document cover,
grasp the cover and slide
it firmly to the left.

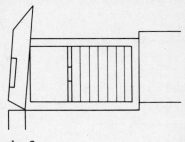

Display 3

ASSUMPTION:

The first page to be
copied is on the glass.

INSTRUCTION:

Press the Start button
(to produce a copy
in the output tray).

THE COPIER

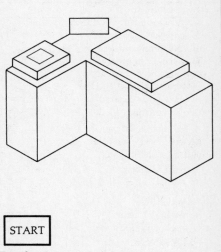

START

Display 4

ASSUMPTION:

The copy of your original
on the glass has been made.

INSTRUCTION:

Slide the document cover right
(to remove the original).

How to open the document cover:

To open the document cover,
grasp the cover and slide
it all the way to the right.

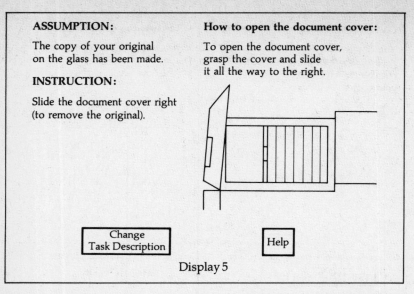

Change
Task Description

Help

Display 5

INSTRUCTION:

Remove the original from the glass.
If more pages are to be
copied, then:

    Place the next page
    face down on the glass.
    Slide the document cover
    left until it latches.

Otherwise, lower the RDH
until it latches.

THE COPIER

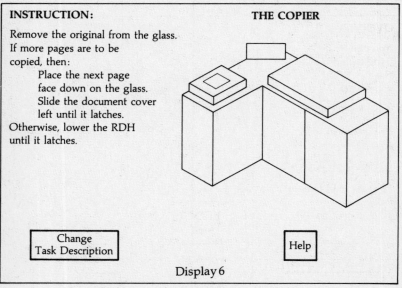

Change
Task Description

Help

Display 6

OVERVIEW:

You can use the Recirculating Document Handler (RDH) to make your copies.

INSTRUCTION:

Place all of your originals in the RDH, first page on top (so that the RDH can automatically feed each sheet into the copier).

THE COPIER

This is the RDH.

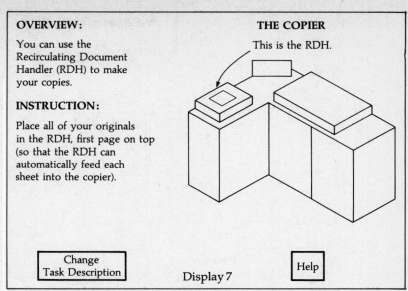

| Change Task Description | Display 7 | Help |

OVERVIEW:

You can use the Recirculating Document Handler (RDH) to make your copies.

ASSUMPTION:

The document to be copied is in the RDH.

INSTRUCTION:

Press the Start button (to produce 4 copies in the output tray).

THE COPIER

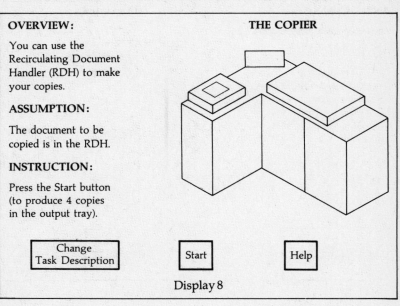

| Change Task Description | Start | Help |

Display 8

ASSUMPTION:

The copies have been made.

INSTRUCTION:

Remove the originals
from the RDH.

THE COPIER

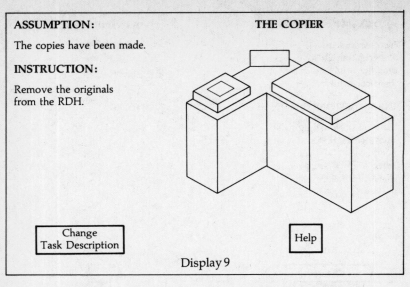

Change
Task Description

Help

Display 9

ASSUMPTION:

The copies have been made

INSTRUCTION:

Remove the copies
from the output tray.

THE COPIER

The output tray is where
the copies come out.
It is located on the right
side and is colored blue.

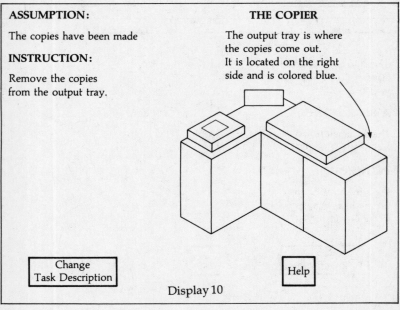

Change
Task Description

Help

Display 10

176

ASSUMPTION:

A copy of your document is being used as the original to make the final copies.

The back sides of the copies have been made.

INSTRUCTION:

Place the copies in the top paper tray.

The COPIER

The top paper tray is to the right of the output paper tray.

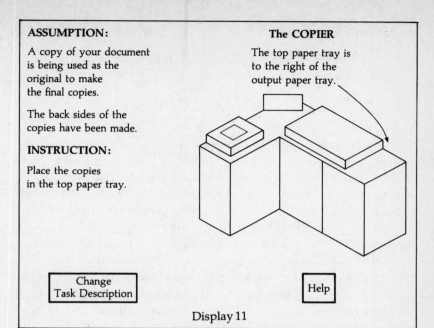

Change
Task Description

Help

Display 11

177

8 Conclusion

The theme of this book has been in one sense an obvious proposition: namely, that insofar as actions are always situated in particular social and physical circumstances, the situation is crucial to action's interpretation. The very obviousness of this fact about action contributes to the ways in which it has been overlooked. The intellectual tradition of the cognitive sciences, in particular applied logic, has taken abstract structural accounts as the ideal representational form. An adequate account of any phenomenon, according to this tradition, is a formal theory that represents just those aspects of the phenomenon that are true regardless of particular circumstances. This relation of abstract structures to particular instances is exemplified in the relation of plans to situated actions. Plans are taken to be either formal structures that control situated actions, or abstractions over instances of situated action, the instances serving to fill in the abstract structure on particular occasions. The research strategy in cognitive science has been to represent mental constructs, such as goals or plans, then stipulate the procedures by which those constructs are realized as action, or recognized as the actor's intent. The specification of procedures for action, in turn, has presupposed enumeration of the conditions under which a given action is appropriate. These stipulated conditions, ready made and coupled to their associated actions, take the place of a lively, moment-by-moment assessment of the significance of particular circumstances.

In contrast to this cognitivist view, I have proposed an alternative approach drawn from recent developments in the social sciences, principally anthropology and sociology. The aim of research, according to this approach, is not to produce formal models of

Conclusion

knowledge and action, but to explore the relation of knowledge and action to the particular circumstances in which knowing and acting invariably occur. This alternative approach requires corresponding changes in the way in which research on purposeful action proceeds. The first is a fundamental change in perspective, such that the contingence of action on a complex world of objects, artifacts, and other actors, located in space and time, is no longer treated as an extraneous problem with which the individual actor must contend, but rather is seen as the essential resource that makes knowledge possible and gives action its sense. The second change is a renewed commitment to grounding theories of action in empirical evidence: that is, to building generalizations inductively from records of particular, naturally occurring activities, and maintaining the theory's accountability to that evidence. Finally, and perhaps most importantly, this approach assumes that the coherence of action is not adequately explained by either preconceived cognitive schema or institutionalized social norms. Rather, the organization of situated action is an emergent property of moment-by-moment interactions between actors, and between actors and the environments of their action.

The emergent properties of action means that it is not predetermined, but neither is it random. A basic research goal for studies of situated action, therefore, is to explicate the relationship between structures of action and the resources and constraints afforded by physical and social circumstances. Ethnomethodology begins from the premise that we need, and have yet to produce, an adequate base of descriptions of situated human practices. Because there is no stable observational base, the social sciences "are talking sciences, and achieve in texts, not elsewhere, the observability and practical objectivity of their phenomena" (Garfinkel, Lynch, and Livingston 1981, p. 133). As Heritage has recently stated the problem:

The "boundaries" of specific, located ordinary actions, their "units" or "segments," the determination of adequacy in their description or representation – all of these questions and many more pose problems which cannot be resolved "in principle" but which require solution in the context of practical engagement with descriptive tasks. (1984, p. 302)

In this study I have attempted to begin constructing a descriptive foundation for the analysis of human–machine communication. A growing corpus of observations from the analysis of everyday human conversation provides a baseline from which to assess the state of interactivity between people and machines. First, the mutual intelligibility that we achieve in our everyday interactions – sometimes with apparent effortlessness, sometimes with obvious travail – is always the product of *in situ*, collaborative work. Secondly, the general communicative practices that support that work are designed to maximize sensitivity to particular participants, on particular occasions of interaction. Thirdly, face-to-face communication includes resources for detecting and remedying troubles in understanding as part of its fundamental organization. And fourthly, every occasion of human communication is embedded in, and makes use of, an unarticulated background of experiences and circumstances. Communication in this sense is not a symbolic process that happens to go on in real-word settings, but a real-world activity in which we make use of language to delineate the collective relevance of our shared environment.

The application of insights gained through research on face-to-face human interaction, in particular conversation analysis, to the study of human–computer interaction promises to be a productive research path. The initial observation is that interaction between people and machines requires essentially the same interpretive work that characterizes interaction between people, but with fundamentally different resources available to the participants. In particular, people make use of a rich array of linguistic, nonverbal, and inferential resources in finding the intelligibility of actions and events, in making their own actions sensible, and in managing the troubles in understanding that inevitably arise. Today's machines, in contrast, rely on a fixed array of sensory inputs, mapped to a pre-determined set of internal states and responses. The result is an asymmetry that substantially limits the scope of interaction between people and machines. Taken seriously, this asymmetry poses three outstanding problems for the design of interactive machines. First, the problem of how to lessen the asymmetry by extending the access of the machine to the actions and circumstances of the user. Secondly, the problem of how to make clear to the user the limits on the machine's access to those basic interactional resources. And finally, the problem of how to find ways of compensating for the machine's lack of access to the user's situation with computationally available alternatives.

8.1 Toward practical solutions

In the design of interactive machines, the most common substitute for access to the user and her situation has been the incorporation into the machine of a preconceived representation of the user and her situation, or a "user model." User models, constructed in advance as the template against which the user's actual actions re mapped, comprise propositions about the domain, the task, the typical user, and the like. Recently, designers concerned with the provison of situated help, or so-called intelligent tutoring systems, have begun extending such models to support local, or "real-time" assessment of the actions of the computer user (see Burton and Brown 1982, London and Clancey 1982, Woolf and McDonald 1983, Farrell, Anderson, and Reiser 1984, Peachey and McCalla 1986, Shrager and Finin 1982). A primary objective of such systems is to infer the user's knowledge and misconceptions about the system by observing her actions, rather than relying on either error conditions or explicit requests for help. To appreciate the requirements of this objective, one has simply to imagine those occasions where an expert, watching a novice engaged in some activity, would be moved to intercede. The outstanding question with respect to this form of coaching is, Just what does seeing those places where assistance is called for, and knowing what needs to be said, involve? Researchers pursuing "real-time user modeling" as the basis for a solution to this problem have adopted the following design strategies:

(1) *Diagnosis based on differential modeling*. A principal strategy for so-called intelligent tutoring systems, or computer-based coaches, has been to work from an ideal model of expert behavior in a given domain, to which the actions of student can be mapped. It is then the *difference* between expert and student behavior in particular circumstances that serves as the basis for assessing the student's knowledge and skills. The diagnosis works both on manifested errors that arise in the course of the student's actions and, more subtly, on the omisson of actions that, given a particular set of conditions, an idealized expert in those circumstances would take. The rationale for the differential modeling strategy is a combination of predictions based on the model of expert behavior, with techniques for local assessment of the student's actions. The success of the strategy turns on the degree of fit between the actions anticipated by the diagnostic model, and the actions of the student that are detectable by the machine.

(2) *Detection of diagnostic inconsistencies*. However felicitous the fit between student actions and diagnostic issues, the design must accommodate the likelihood of misdiagnosis, and provide for its detection and repair. In the best intelligent tutoring systems, the accumulating record of student actions includes both actions that manifest some issue which according to the current diagnosis should not appear, and actions that fail to manifest some issue that the student seems from prior diagnosis to understand. Evidence of misdiagnosis is found in the amount of "tear," or inconsistency, in the accumulating record of student actions.[1] When the disparity

---

[1] The notion of "tear," and many other subtleties now beginning to be incorporated in the design of computer-based coaches, originates in Burton and Brown's work on WEST (1982).

between the developing diagnostic model of what the student knows and doesn't know, and the understanding demonstrated in subsequent actions, reaches a certain threshold, the program may invoke alternative strategies that the student might be using. Possible alternative strategies, identified according to local evidence, are then tested for consistency with the global history of the student's actions. Crucially, the domain must be sufficiently closed that the set of possible alternative strategies can be enumerated.

(3) *Separation of local and global interpretations.* Recent tutoring systems begin to make use of a mechanism basic to everyday human communication, namely the separation, and productive interaction, between local and global interpretations of the other's actions. The diagnosis of student actions in computer-based tutoring systems is accomplished through two independent though interrelated mechanisms: one component which is data-driven from the local context of a given action, and another which runs over an accumulating history of the student's actions with the goal of identifying weaknesses or misunderstandings. As in the interpretation of action in the course of a developing conversation, it is the interaction of these two perspectives that affords the power of the diagnosis. The locality of the data-driven component supports an assessment of each particular action, relatively unconstrained by global preconceptions, while the global perspective of the evaluative component supports the interpretation of that action as a reflection of the student's general strategies and skills.

(4) *The constructive use of trouble.* In much the way that ordinary conversation relies upon the successful detection, repair, and even exploitation of troubles in understanding, recent tutoring systems adopt a "constructivist position" towards errors, such that the inevitability of student misconceptions or weaknesses is turned to pedagogical advantage.[2] The goal of the coach in such systems is

---

[2] Again, the introduction of this position into the design of computer-based instruction is due to Burton and Brown (1982).

not to avoid student errors, but to make them accessible to the student, and therefore instructive. If the student has enough information to identify and repair an error, then it is considered a constructive one. If, on the other hand, the error is not manifest in such a way as to be visible, or is perceived but the student lacks the necessary information for its repair, the trouble is non-constructive. One major task of the coach, on this view, is to give the student the information required to transform non-constructive troubles into constructive ones, either by diagnosing the trouble and making it accessible, or by providing the information required for its repair.

This last strategy has recently been generalized as a call to design for the management of trouble (see Brown and Newman 1985). Such an objective implies at least that users are encouraged to use the wider social setting in which a machine is embedded as a resource to remedy the troubles in understanding that inevitably arise. Applied to the design of machines, it recommends incorporating the kind of diagnostic and interactional abilities that characterize the human coach into the machine itself. The problem in applying this later recommendation is that often the "grain size" of machine-readable actions is either too small or too large to constrain the analysis of the user's actions adequately. So, for example, in the case of the help system described in chaper 7, to appreciate the significance of a given user action – say, putting a document into the document handler – may require reference to a history that extends across procedures as the system tracks them. Alternatively, assessing the user's actions may require reference to sub-procedures, such as ordering pages of a document correctly, for which there is no trace. In general, if there is more than one understanding that can produce what appears to be the same action, detecting the action does not serve as unequivocal evidence that the understanding is actually in hand. By the same token, if a given skill can be manifest in some indefinite number of different actions, then the absence of an expected action does not necessarily mean the absence of the skill. While in the case of the human coach these ambiguities are resolved through interaction, in the case of a computer-based coach the limits on the machine's access pose a difficult design problem. The problem is not simply that communicative troubles arise that do not arise in human communication, but rather that when the inevitable troubles do arise, there are not the same resources available for their detection and repair.

8.2 Plans as resources for action

Some researchers in human–computer interaction make the claim that cognitive science and computer technologies have advanced to the point where it is now feasible to build instructional computer systems that are as effective as experienced human tutors (see, for example, Anderson, Boyle, and Reiser 1985). In contrast to this optimism, I have argued that there is a profound and persisting asymmetry in interaction between people and machines, due to a disparity in their relative access to the moment-by-moment contingencies that constitute the conditions of situated interaction. Because of the asymmetry of user and machine, interface design is less a project of simulating human communication than of engineering alternatives to interaction's situated properties.

The primary alternative has been to substitute a generalized representation of the situation of action for access to the unique details of the user's particular situation. As in the expert help system analyzed in chapter 7, the representational scheme favored by many designers has been the *plan*. The problem for designers is that, as common-sense formulations of intent, plans are inherently vague. To the cognitive scientist, this representational vagueness is a fault to be remedied, insofar as a plan is the prerequisite for purposeful action, and the details of action are derived from the completion and modification of the plan. The task of the designer who would model situated action, therefore, is to improve upon, or render more precise and axiomatic, the plan.

For situated action, however, the vagueness of plans is not a fault, but is ideally suited to the fact that the detail of intent and action must be contingent on the circumstantial and interactional particulars of actual situations. Given this view of plans, namely as resources for action rather than as controlling structures, the outstanding problem is not to improve upon them, but to understand what kind of resource they are. The most promising approach is to begin from the observation that plans are representations, or abstractions over action. In one sense, this simply joins the problem of plans to the more general, and no less difficult, question of representation. But in another sense, viewing plans as representations is suggestive of what their relation to unrepresented actions might be.

Chapter 4 introduced a view, developed recently by Barwise and Perry (1985), that language can be characterized in terms of its *efficiency* and *indexicality*. By efficiency is meant simply the ways in which "expressions used by different people, in different space-time locations, with different connections to the world around them, can have different interpretations, even though they retain the same linguistic meaning" (p. 5). In its efficiency, language provides us with a shareable resource for talk about the world. At the same time, the efficiency of language requires that our utterances always be anchored to the unique and particular occasions of their use. In this respect, language is indexical: that is, dependent for its significance on connections to particular occasions, and to the concrete circumstances in which an utterance is spoken. This view of language is taken as foundational by Garfinkel (1967), and by Garfinkel and Sacks (1970) with respect to the intelligibility and significance of action.

Like other essentially linguistic representations, plans are efficient formulations of situated actions. By abstracting uniformities across situations, plans allow us to bring past experience and projected outcomes to bear on our present actions. As efficient formulations, however, the significance of plans turns on their relation back to the unique circumstances and unarticulated practices of situated activities. A problem for an account of situated action, on this view, is to describe the processes by which efficient

representations are brought into productive interaction with particular actions in particular environments. A rich description of this
process comes, for example, from research on Micronesian navigation reported by Edwin Hutchins (1983). The natives of the Caroline
Islands routinely embark on ocean-going canoe voyages that take
them several days out of the sight of land. Western researchers trav-
elling with them have found that, at any time during the voyage,
the navigators can indicate the bearings of the port of departure,
the target island, and other islands off to the side of the course they
are steering, even though these may all be over the horizon and out
of sight. They are able to do this and other feats of navigation that
are simply impossible for a Western navigator without instru-
ments. What Hutchins reports is that they maintain their course by
substituting other environmental referents, that are accessible, for
the inaccessible land. In particular, they follow a star path, selected
with reference to a sidereal compass or star chart that forms a map
between pairs of islands. To maintain their orientation to the star
path at any given point in their voyage requires that they consult
not only the stars, but a rich set of changing environmental circumstances – the color of the water, the waves, winds and clouds,
birds, and so forth – which through experience become interpretable for information about the relative position of the canoe. What
is notable about Hutchins's account of the resources of the Micronesian navigator is that nowhere is a preconceived plan in evidence.
The basis for navigation seems to be, instead, local interactions
with the environment. In this way, navigators maintain their orientation to the star path, which in turn is fixed to the islands of origin
and destination.

The Micronesian example demonstrates how the nature of an activity can be missed unless one views purposeful action as an interaction between a representation and the particular contingent
details of the environment. With respect to plans and actions, Feitelson and Stefik (1977) found this same relation present in the
work of geneticists planning scientific experiments. Specifically,
they found that geneticists elaborated their plans only far enough

to act as a framework in which to organize the constraints of the laboratory. Rather than planning the experiment through an *a priori* analysis, the experimenters decided what to do next by relating each current observation to their research goals. The experimenters' expertise lay not in completing the plan, but in the ability to generate hypotheses continually, and to exploit serendipity in the course of the experiment. The experimental process, being what Feitelson and Stefik call "event driven," allowed the experimenter to "fish for interesting possibilities"; that is, to follow up on unanticipated observations and opportunities provided by a particular experimental set-up.

From these and other examples, we can begin to draw an alternative account of the relation of plans to situated actions. The foundation of actions by this account is not plans, but local interactions with our environment, more and less informed by reference to abstract representations of situations and of actions, and more and less available to representation themselves. The function of abstract representations is not to serve as specifications for the local interactions, but rather to orient or position us in a way that will allow us, through local interactions, to exploit some contingencies of our environment, and to avoid others. While plans *can be* elaborated indefinitely, they elaborate actions just to the level that elaboration is useful; they are vague with respect to the details of action precisely at the level at which it makes sense to forego abstract representation, and rely on the availability of a particular, embodied response.

The interesting problem for an account of action, finally, is not to improve upon common-sense plans, but to describe how it is that we are able to bring efficient descriptions (such as plans) and particular circumstances into productive interaction. The assumption in planning research in cognitive science has been that this process consists in filling in the details of the plan to some operational level. But when we look at actual studies of situated action, it seems that situated action turns on local interactions between the actor and contingencies that, while they are made accountable to a plan, remain essentially outside of the plan's scope. Just as it would seem absurd to claim that a map in some strong sense controlled the traveler's movements through the world, it is wrong to imagine plans as controlling actions. On the other hand, the question of how a map is produced for specific purposes, how in any actual instance it is interpreted *vis-à-vis* the world, and how its use is a resource for traversing the world, is a reasonable and productive one. In the last analysis, it is in the interaction of representation and represented where, so to speak, the action is. To get at the action *in situ* requires accounts not only of efficient symbolic representations but of their productive interaction with the unique, unrepresented circumstances in which action in every instance and invariably occurs.

A starting premise of this book was that the project of building interactive machines has more to gain by understanding the differences between human interaction and machine operation, than by simply assuming their similarity. My argument has been that as long as machine actions are determined by stipulated conditions, machine interaction with the world, and with people in particular, will be limited to the intentions of designers and their ability to anticipate and constrain the user's actions. The generality of various representations of situations and actions is the principle resource for this task, while the context insensitivity of such representational schemes is the principle limitation. The question, finally, is: What are the consequences of that limitation? The answer will differ according to whether our concern is with practical or with theoretical consequences. Practically, ingenious design combined with testing may do much to extend the range of useful machine behavior. Theoretically, understanding the limits of machine behavior challenges our understanding of the resources of human action. Just as the project of building intelligent artifacts has been enlisted in the service of a theory of mind, the attempt to build interactive artifacts, taken seriously, could contribute much to an account of situated human action and shared understanding.

References

Allen, J.   1983.   Recognizing intentions from natural language utterances. In *Computational Models of Discourse*, M. Brady and R. Berwick, eds., ch. 2. Cambridge, MA: MIT Press.

1984.   Towards a general theory of action and time. *Artificial Intelligence* 23:123–54.

Amerine, R. and Bilmes, J.   1979.   Following instruction. Unpublished manuscript, University of California, Santa Barbara.

Anderson, J., Boyle, C., and Reiser, B.   1985.   Intelligent tutoring systems. *Science* 228: 456–62.

Anscombe, G. E. M.   1957.   *Intentions*. Oxford: Basil Blackwell.

Appelt, D.   1985.   Planning English referring expressions. *Artificial Intelligence* 26: 1–33.

Atkinson, J. M. and Drew, P.   1979.   *Order in Court: The Organization of Verbal Interaction in Judicial Settings*. Atlantic Highlands, NJ: Humanities Press.

Austin, J. L.   1962.   *How to do Things with Words*. Oxford: Clarendon Press.

Barwise, J. and Perry, J.   1985.   *Situations and Attitudes*. Cambridge, MA: MIT Press.

Bates, E.   1976.   *Language and Context: The Acquisition of Pragmatics*. New York, NY: Academic Press.

Beckman, H. and Frankel, R.   1983.   Who hides the agenda: the impact of physician behavior on the collection of data. Presented to the Fourth Annual SREPCIM Task Force on Interviewing, Washington, DC, April 1983. [Address reprint requests to Howard Beckman, MD, POD 5C, University Health Center, 4201 St Antoine, Detroit, MI 48201.]

Berreman, G.   1966.   Anemic and emetic analyses in social anthroplogy. *American Anthropologist* 68(2)1:346–54.

Birdwhistell, R.   1970.   *Kinesics and Context: Essays on Body Motion Communication*. Philadelphia, PA: University of Pennsylvania Press.

Blumer, H.   1969.   *Symbolic Interactionism*. Englewood Cliffs, NJ: Prentice-Hall.

References

Bobrow, D. G., Kaplan, R. M., Kay, M., Norman, D. A., Thompson, H., and Winograd, T. 1977. GUS: a frame-driven dialogue system. *Artificial Intelligence* 8: 155–73.

Boden, M. 1973. The structure of intentions. *Journal of Theory of Social Behavior* 3:23–46.

Brady, M. and Berwick, R. (eds.) 1983. *Computational Models of Discourse*. Cambridge, MA: MIT Press.

Brown, J. S. and Newman, S. 1985. Issues in cognitive and social ergonomics: from our house to Bauhaus. *Human–Computer Interaction* 1:359–91.

Brown, J. S., Rubenstein, R., and Burton, R. 1976. *Reactive Learning Environment for Computer Assisted Electronics Instruction*. BBN Report 3314, Bolt Beranek and Newman, Inc., Cambridge, MA.

Bruce, B. 1981. Natural communication between person and computer. In *Strategies for Natural Language Processing*, W. Lehnert and M. Ringle, eds. Hillsdale, NJ: Erlbaum.

Bruner, J. 1986. *Actual Minds, Possible Worlds*. Cambridge, MA: Harvard University Press.

Burke, J. 1982. An analysis of intelligibility in a practical activity. Unpublished Ph.D. dissertation, University of Illinois at Urbana–Champaign.

Burton, R. and Brown, J. S. 1982. An investigation of computer coaching for informal learning activities. In *Intelligent Tutoring Systems*, D. Sleeman and J. S. Brown, eds. London: Academic Press.

Carbonell, J. R. 1971. *Mixed-Initiative Man–Computer Dialogues*. Technical Report 1970, Bolt Beranek and Newman, Inc., Cambridge, MA.

Carey, S. 1985. *Conceptual Change in Childhood*. Cambridge, MA: MIT Press.

Churchland, P. 1984. *Matter and Consciousness*. Cambridge, MA: MIT Press.

Cohen, J. 1966. *Human Robots in Myth and Science*. London: Allen and Unwin.

Cohen, P. [n.d.] Pragmatics, speaker-reference, and the modality of communication. Unpublished manuscript, Laboratory for Artificial Intelligence, Fairchild Camera and Instrument Corp., Palo Alto, CA.

Cohen, P. and Perrault, C. R. 1979. Elements of a plan-based theory of speech acts. *Cognitive Science* 3:177–212.

Colby, K. M. *et al.* 1972. Turing-like indistinguishability tests for the validation of a computer simulation of paranoid processes. *Artificial Intelligence* 3:199–221.

References

Coombs, M. and Alty, J. 1984. Expert systems: an alternative paradigm. *International Journal of Man–Machine Studies* 20:21–43.

Coulter, J. 1979. *The Social Construction of Mind*. Totowa, NJ: Rowman and Littlefield.

1983. *Rethinking Cognitive Theory*. New York, NY: St. Martin's Press.

Dennett, D. 1978. *Brainstorms*. Cambridge, MA: MIT Press.

Dreyfus, H. 1979. *What Computers Can't Do: The Limits of Artificial Intelligence*, revised edition. New York, NY: Harper and Row.

(ed.) 1982. *Husserl Intentionality and Cognitive Science*. Cambridge, MA: MIT Press.

In press. *Being-in-the-world: A Commentary on Heidegger's Being and Time, Division I*. Cambridge, MA: MIT Press.

Duncan, S. Jr. 1974. On the structure of speaker–auditor interaction during speaking turns. *Language in Society* 3:161–80.

Durkheim, E. 1938. *The Rules of Sociological Method*. New York, NY: The Free Press.

Erickson, F. 1982. Money tree, lasagna bush, salt and pepper: social construction of topical cohesion in a conversation among Italian-Americans. In *Georgetown University Round Table on Language and Linguistics: Analyzing Discourse: Text and Talk*, D. Tannen, ed. Washington, DC: Georgetown University Press.

Erickson, F. and Shultz, J. 1982. *The Counselor as Gatekeeper*. New York, NY: Academic Press.

Farrell, R., Anderson, J., and Reiser, B. 1984. An interactive computer-based tutor for LISP. *Proceedings of the American Association for Artificial Intelligence*, pp. 106–9. Austin, TX.

Feitelson, J. and Stefik, M. 1977. A case study of the reasoning in a genetics experiment. *Heuristic Programming Project*, Working Paper 77-18, Stanford, CA: Stanford University.

Fikes, R. and Nilsson, N. 1971. STRIPS: a new approach to the application of theorem proving to problem solving. *Artificial Intelligence* 2: 189–205.

Fitter, M. 1979. Towards more "natural" interactive systems. *International Journal of Man–Machine Studies* 11:339–49.

Fodor, J. 1983. *The Modularity of Mind*. Cambridge, MA: MIT Press.

Frankel, R. 1984. From sentence to sequence: understanding the medical encounter through microinteractional analysis. *Discourse Processes* 7:135–70.

Galaty, J. 1981. Models and metaphors: on the semiotic explanation of segmentary systems. In *The Structure of Folk Models*, L. Holy and M. Stuchlik, eds. New York: Academic Press.

References

Gardner, H.   1985.   *The Mind's New Science*. New York: Basic Books.

Garfinkel, H.   1967.   *Studies in Ethnomethodology*. Englewood Cliffs, NJ: Prentice-Hall.

   1972.   Remarks on ethnomethodology. In *Directions in Sociolinguistics: The Ethnography of Communication*, J. Gumperz and D. Hymes, eds. New York, NY: Holt, Rinehart and Winston.

Garfinkel, H. and Sacks, H.   1970.   On formal structures of practical actions. In *Theoretical Sociology*, J. McKinney and E. Tiryakian, eds. New York, NY: Appleton-Century-Crofts.

Garfinkel, H., Lynch, M., and Livingston, E.   1981.   The work of a discovering science construed with materials from the optically discovered pulsar. *Philosophy of the Social Sciences* 11:131–58.

Geertz, C.   1973.   *The Interpretation of Cultures*. New York, NY: Basic Books.

Gladwin, T.   1964.   Culture and logical process. In *Explorations in Cultural Anthropology: Essays Presented to George Peter Murdock*, W. Goodenough, ed. New York, NY: McGraw-Hill.

Goffman, E.   1975.   Replies and responses. *Language in Society* 5:257–313.

Goodwin, C.   1981.   *Conversational Organization: Interaction Between Speakers and Hearers*. New York, NY: Academic Press.

Goodwin, M.   1980.   Processes of mutual monitoring implicated in the production of description sequences. *Sociological Inquiry* 50:303–17.

Grice, H. P.   1975.   Logic and conversation. In *Syntax and Semantics*, vol. 3: *Speech Acts*, P. Cole and J. Morgan, eds. New York, NY: Academic Press.

Grosz, B.   1981.   Focusing and description in natural language dialogues. In *Elements of Discourse Understanding*, Joshi, A., Webber, B., and Sag, I., eds. Cambridge University Press.

Gumperz, J.   1982a   *Discourse Strategies*. Cambridge: Cambridge University Press.

   1982b. The linguistic bases of communicative competence. In *Georgetown University Round Table on Language and Linguistics: Analyzing Discourse: Text and Talk*, D. Tannen, ed. Washington, DC: Georgetown University Press.

Gumperz, J. and Tannen, D.   1979.   Individual and social differences in language use. In *Individual Differences in Language Ability and Language Behavior*, C. Fillmore *et al.*, eds. New York: Academic Press.

Hayes, P.   1981.   A construction-specific approach to focused interaction in flexible parsing. *Proceedings of Nineteenth Annual Meeting of the Association for Computational Linguistics*, pp. 149–52. Stanford, CA: Stanford University.

References

Hayes, P. and Reddy, D. R.   1983.   Steps toward graceful interaction in spoken and written man–machine communication. *International Journal of Man–Machine Studies* 19:231–84.

Heap, J.   1980.   Description in ethnomethodology. *Human Studies* 3:87–106.

Hendrix, G. G.   1977.   Human engineering for applied natural language processing. *Proceedings of the Fifth International Joint Conference on Artificial Intelligence*, pp. 183–91. Cambridge MA: MIT.

Heritage, J.   1984.   *Garfinkel and Ethnomethodology*. Cambridge, England: Polity Press.

   1985. Recent developments in conversation analysis. *Sociolinguistics* 15:1–16.

Hutchins, E.   1983.   Understanding Micronesian navigation. In *Mental Models*, D. Gentner, and A. Stevens, eds. Hillsdale, NJ: Erlbaum.

Jefferson, G.   1972.   Side sequences. In *Studies in Social Interaction*, D. Sudnow, ed. New York: Free Press.

   1983.   Issues in the transcription of naturally occurring talk: caricature versus capturing pronunciational particulars. *Tilburg Papers in Language and Literature*, no. 34, Tilburg University, Tilburg, The Netherlands.

Jordan, B. and Fuller, N.   1975.   On the non-fatal nature of trouble: sense-making and trouble-managing in *Lingua Franca* talk. *Semiotica* 13:1–31.

Joshi, A., Webber, B., and Sag, I. (eds.)   1981.   *Elements of Discourse Understanding*. Cambridge University Press.

Levinson, S.   1983.   *Pragmatics*. Cambridge University Press.

London, B. and Clancey, W.   1982.   Plan recognition strategies in student modeling: prediction and description. *Proceedings of the American Association for Artificial Intelligence*, pp. 335–8. Pittsburgh, PA.

Lynch, M.   1985.   *Art and Artifact in Laboratory Science*. London: Routledge and Kegan Paul.

Lynch, M., Livingston, E., and Garfinkel, H.   1983.   Temporal order in laboratory work. In *Science Observed*, K. Knorr and M. Mulkay, eds. London: Sage.

McCorduck, P.   1979.   *Machines Who Think*. San Francisco, CA: W. H. Freeman.

McDermott, R.   1976.   Kids make sense: an ethnographic account of the interactional management of success and failure in one first-grade classroom. Unpublished Ph.D. dissertation, Stanford University.

MacKay, D. M.   1962.   The use of behavioral language to refer to mechanical processes. *British Journal of Philosophical Science*, 13:89–103.

References

Mead, G. H. 1934. *Mind, Self, and Society*. University of Chicago Press.

Merritt, M. 1977. On questions following questions in service encounters. *Language in Society* 5:315–57.

Miller, G., Galanter, E., and Pribram, K. 1960. *Plans and the Structure of Behavior*. New York, NY: Holt, Rinehart and Winston.

Newell, A. and Simon, H. 1972. *Human Problem Solving*. Englewood Cliffs, NJ: Prentice-Hall.

Nickerson, R. 1976. On conversational interaction with computers. In *Proceedings of ACM/SIGGRAPH workshop*, October 14–15, pp. 101–13. Pittsburgh, PA.

Nilsson, N. 1973. A hierarchical robot planning and execution system. In *Technical Note 76*, SRI Artificial Intelligence Center, Stanford Research Institute, April. Menlo Park, CA.

Oberquelle, H., Kupka, I., and Maass, S. 1983. A view of human–machine communication and cooperation. *International Journal of Man–Machine Studies* 19:309–33.

Ochs, E. 1979. Planned and unplanned discourse. In *Syntax and Semantics*, vol. 12: *Discourse and Syntax*, T. Givon, ed. New York, NY: Academic Press.

Peachey, D. and McCalla, G. 1986. Using planning techniques in intelligent tutoring systems. *International Journal of Man–Machine Studies* 24:77–98.

Peirce, C. 1933. *Collected Papers*, vol II, C. Hartshorne and P. Weiss, eds. Cambridge, MA: Harvard University Press.

Pylyshyn, Z. 1974. Minds, machines and phenomenology: some reflections on Dreyfus' *What Computers Can't Do*. *Cognition* 3:57–77.

1984. *Computation and Cognition*. Cambridge, MA: MIT Press.

Rubin, A. 1980. A theoretical taxonomy of the differences between oral and written language. In *Theoretical Issues in Reading Comprehension*, R. Spiro *et al*. eds. Hillsdale, NJ: Erlbaum.

Sacerdoti, E. 1975. The nonlinear nature of plans. *Proceedings of the Fourth International Joint Conference on Artificial Intelligence*. Tbilisi, USSR.

1977. *A Structure for Plans and Behavior*. New York, NY: Elsevier.

Sacks, H. 1963. Sociological description. *Berkeley Journal of Sociology* 8:1–16.

1974. An analysis of the course of a joke's telling in conversation. In *Explorations in the Ethnography of Speaking*, R. Bauman and J. Scherzer, eds. Cambridge University Press.

Sacks, H., Schegloff, E., and Jefferson, G. 1978. A simplest systematics for the organization of turn-taking in conversation. In *Studies in the*

Organization of Conversational Interaction, J. Schenkein, ed. New York, NY: Academic Press.

Schank, R. and Abelson, R. 1977. Scripts, plans and knowledge. In *Thinking: Readings in Cognitive Science*, P. Johnson-Laird and P. Wason, eds. Cambridge University Press.

Scheflen, A. E. 1974. *How Behavior Means*. Garden City, NY.: Anchor Press.

Schegloff, E. 1972. Sequencing in conversational openings. In *Directions in Sociolinguistics: The Ethnography of Communication*, J. Gumperz and D. Hymes, eds. New York, NY: Academic Press.

1982. Discourse as an interactional achievement: some uses of "uh huh" and other things that come between sentences. In *Georgetown University Round Table on Language and Linguistics: Analyzing Discourse: Text and Talk*, D. Tannen, ed. Washington, DC: Georgetown University Press.

Schegloff, E. and Sachs, H. 1973. Opening up closings. *Semiotica* 7:289–327.

Schmidt, C. F., Sridharan, N., and Goodson, J. 1978. The plan recognition problem. *Artificial Intelligence* 11:45–83.

Schutz, A. 1962. *Collected Papers I: The Problem of Social Reality*. The Hague: Martinus Nijhoff.

Searle, J. 1969. *Speech Acts: An Essay in the Philosophy of Language*. Cambridge University Press.

1979. *Expression and Meaning*. Cambridge University Press.

1980. The intentionality of intention and action. *Cognitive Science* 4:47–70.

Shrager, J. and Finin, T. 1982. An expert system that volunteers advice. *Proceedings of the American Association for Artificial Intelligence*, pp. 339–40. Pittsburgh, PA.

Sidner, C. L. 1979. Towards a computational theory of definite anaphora comprehension in English discourse. *Technical Report TR–537*, MIT AI Laboratory. Cambridge, MA.

Stich, S. 1983. *From Folk Psychology to Cognitive Science*. Cambridge, MA: MIT Press.

Streeck, J. 1980. Speech acts in interaction: a critique of Searle. *Discourse Processes* 3: 133–54.

Suchman, L. 1982. Toward a sociology of human–machine interaction: pragmatics of instruction-following. CIS Working Paper, Palo Alto, CA: Xerox Palo Alto Research Center.

Turing, A. M. 1950. Computing machinery and intelligence. *Mind* 59(236):433–61.

References

Turkle, S. 1984. *The Second Self.* New York, NY: Simon and Schuster.

Turner, R. 1962. Words, utterances and activities. In *Ethnomethodology: Selected readings*, ed. Turner. Harmondsworth, Middlesex: Penguin.

Watt, W. C. 1968. Habitability. *American Documentation* 19(3):338–51.

Weizenbaum, J. 1983. ELIZA: a computer program for the study of natural language communication between man and machine. *Communications of the ACM, 25th Anniversary Issue*, 26(1):23–7. (Reprinted from *Communications of the ACM*, 29(1):36–45, January 1966.)

Wilson, T. 1970. Conceptions of interaction and forms of sociological explanation. *American Sociological Review* 35:697–709.

Woolf, B. and McDonald, D. 1983. Human–computer discourse in the design of a PASCAL tutor. *Proceedings of the Computer–Human Interaction Conference*, pp. 230–4. Boston, MA.

Zimmerman, D. 1970. The practicalities of rule use. In *Understanding Everyday Life*, J. Douglas, ed. Chicago, II: Aldine.

Author index

Subject index

adjacency pairs, 78–82, 155
agenda, 88, 91–5
anticipation of designer, 132, 134–5, 137–9, 166, 169, 189; *see also* design of interactive machines
artifacts, 4, ch. 2, 132, 189
artificial intelligence research, 6n, 9, 27, 30, 33, 35, 35n, 36, 40, 45, 104, 115n
automata and cognitive science, 7–10

background knowledge, 28, 42–8, 61, 180
batch processing, 11
behaviorism, 8–9, 50, 55

coaching: computer based, 19–21, 19n, 181–4; human, 17, 18–20, 19n, 105–6, 142, 184–5; *see also* expert help systems; instructions to user
cognition, 5, 6n, 8, 9; as computation, 9
cognitive science, ix, 2, 7–10, 27, 37, 43, 47, 48, 61, 67, 70, 101, 178, 185, 188
common sense: knowledge, 43, 45; plans, 49, 188; psychology, 16; view of world, 57–8
communication, 3, 6, 6n, 12–13, 18, 19, 33–6, 40, 45–6, 57, 61–2, 63, 66, 69–71, 86, 95, 115, 118, 119–21, 122–4, 127, 144, 146–8, 155–8, 169–70, 180, 189; situated communication, 4, 33, 70–1, 77; *see also* human–machine communication
communicative economy, 45
communicative resources, ch. 5, 104f.
Computer-Based Consultant project, 104–5
computer model of intelligent behavior, 2–3, 9
conditional relevance, 78, 80, 82–3, 143–69

contextualization cues, 72
conversation analysis, 69, 72–83; notation for, 96–7
cooperation, 41
"cultural dope," 55

deixis, 58, 60, 168
design of interactive machines, 1–2, 4, 5–6, 7, 17, 17n, 18, 19, 21, 98, 99, 100n, 116, 119, 120, 121, 122, 127, 132–4, 143–4, 151–2, 165, 168–9, 170, 181–4, 185, 189; *see also* anticipation of designer
DOCTOR, 23–4, 24n, 65–6
documentary method of interpretation, 23, 63–7

ELIZA, 22–5, 64
ensemble work, 70–2, 180
environment of action, 9, 30, 32–3, 54–6, 68, 179, 180, 187–8; *see also* world model
error response, 32, 102
ethnographic anthropology, *see* social sciences
ethnomethodology, 49–50, 57–8, 62–7, 179
execution monitoring, 29–33
expectations, user's, 12, 13, 148, 163–4, 165, 169–70
expert behavior, viii, 18, 20, 31, 91, 103, 182
expert help systems, 54, 98, 99–101, 106–9, 110n, 111, 114, ch. 7, 185; *see also* instructions to user; coaching
expert systems, 10, 98

"failure and surprise," 30
false alarm, 121, 163–5, 170
feedback, 11, 30, 32

201